I0709700

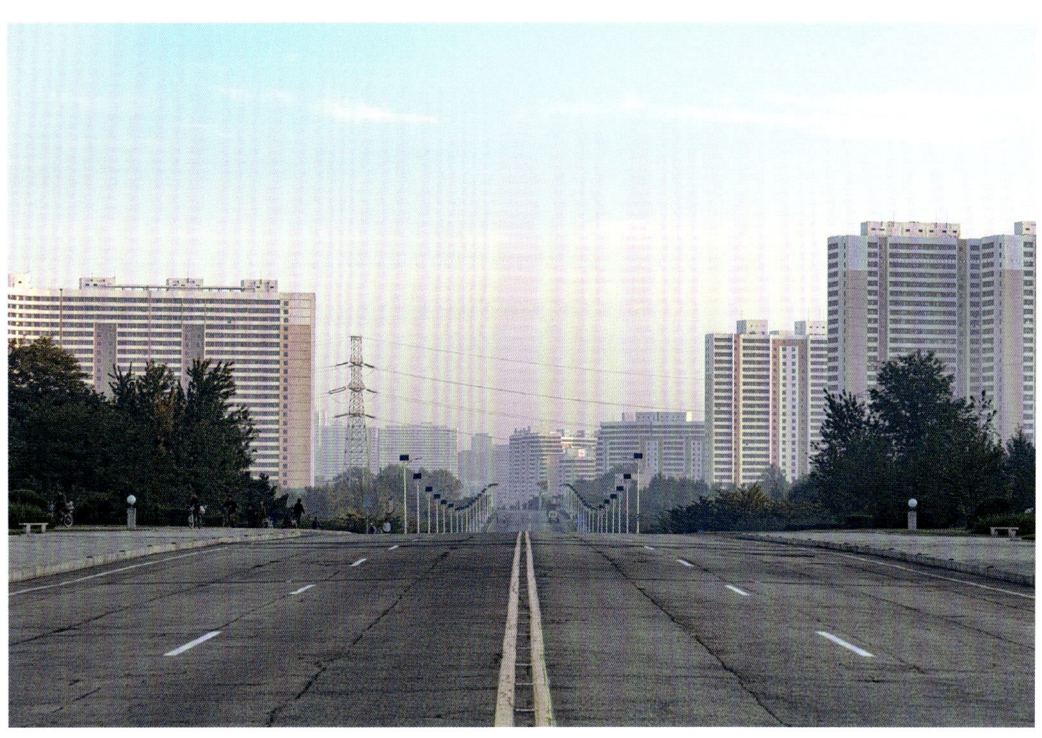

Cofounders: Taj Forer and Michael Itkoff
Creative Director: Ursula Damm
Copy Editor: Gabrielle Fastman

ISBN: 978-1-942084-95-2

Printed by OFSET YAPIMEVI, Turkey

Daylight Books
E-mail: info@daylightbooks.org
Web: www.daylightbooks.org

TED LAU

BETWEEN
DOORS

Words by
Zahra Amiruddin

Daylight

I saw flowers blooming too,
in the fields of an alien land,
but none so pretty
as the flowers of my country.
Vast is the world I looked around,
but best is the country I call mine.
I'd drink a cup of water,
offered by a foreign friend,
but never did it taste sweeter
than spring water of my home.
Vast is the world I looked around,
but best is the country I call mine.

*To my parents,
Robert and Anita*

INTRODUCTION

North Korea, the bad boy of international politics. On a near weekly basis, you will hear news of the country's misbehavior. It might involve a missile launch, or delinquencies on their promise to denuclearize; there is no lack of bad press on the DPRK. However, I have been fascinated by this country since I was young. The likely spark of this fascination was the sight of Andreas Gursky's photographs of the country in all their large-format glory, depicting something so beautiful and so drastically different, I decided I would go and see it all for myself one day. That day came in October 2019.

I believe a vital reason for traveling is to see things that are different from your norm. To explore places and cultures that are not familiar, and see what there is to learn from them. This is why I always look for places that are as different from Hong Kong as possible. North Korea is particularly interesting in that it is a place that is completely shut off from the outside world. Like the Galapagos, with its unique ecosystem and armies of iguanas, North Korea has evolved its own culture over the years. This is the biggest social experiment of its kind on the planet. The result, good or bad, will be a feast for the mind and the eyes.

One thing I have learned over time is that the narrative of Western media can be quite one-sided at times. I can't say it's always wrong, but I do believe it is important to look at things from different perspectives and keep an open mind on issues you do not have first-hand information on. I went to North Korea without any prejudices except a mild uneasiness for my personal safety and I believe others should do the same. Don't pass judgment until you have seen and heard with your own eyes and ears.

The title of the book, *Between Doors*, reflects how it feels to visit North Korea. You are through its borders, yet, still, there is another space that you can't get through. What you can see is still obscured. Despite that, it is possible to get an idea of what things are like for North Koreans. After my journey, I had an uneasy feeling hanging over me. I could not put a finger on it until, one day, I came to the realization that what troubled me was that the citizens of North Korea are not the masters of their fate. I felt an immense sadness that they could not work and strive for the lives they want. For those of us lucky enough to be born into societies with freedom and mobility, opportunity is abundant. There is no limit to your growth but your own imagination. For North Koreans, in all the work they do and all the minutes they live, their potential has been capped by an official, somewhere. What one can achieve is pre-determined by the state. There is no understanding of the meaning of freedom, and I believe there is great cruelty in depriving people of that. Though, in a weird way, it might actually be easier to find happiness in a country like North Korea. In that perfectly curated bubble the citizens live in, as long as they are willing to trust that others have their best interests in mind, it may be possible to have peace and joy. Ignorance can be bliss. But how would you choose?

What I offer you here is my perspective of North Korea. This is a beautiful land, and a land with a beautiful people. The place may be strange, but that doesn't make it a lesser country to any other. Yes, it is being held back by its political system and nuclear ambitions, but its people are not responsible for that. So let's turn our eyes from politics. My wish is for you to see what the lives of the North Korean people are like. To show how ordinary all of this is for them. We all have the same basic needs. We all have the same want for happiness and comfort. North Koreans are just as human as you and I are. I hope this glimpse into their lives will open your mind on this country and show you that it is not just about what you see in the news. It is an immensely interesting place, and how it develops from here is anyone's guess.

—Ted Lau

FOREWORD

Before going to North Korea, Ted and I had traveled to several countries together, and watching him shoot had always fascinated me. In his process, from shooting to editing, he is constantly challenging himself and thinking outside the box. Knowing him as a person and as an artist, I believe it is his personality that makes his work successful. He is determined yet relaxed, precise yet spontaneous.

When we travel, he will often stop at some random spot. I'll look around and wonder, "What's there to see?" The result is always a pleasant surprise. Whenever Ted is shooting, he is extremely focused, as if the lens has sucked him in and the frame is the only world he exists in. Sometimes he'll set his camera up and wait hours for the right moment to happen, but if his vision does not materialize after hours of waiting, he will shrug and simply walk away. Once, after a long wait, I got a bit upset that he was not able to get the result he wanted. He told me, "That's life. We don't always get what we want. There will be more moments that are as great, or even greater." Sometimes he will pick up his camera and take one quick shot of an interesting scene. I once asked him why he didn't take more shots. He told me, "There's no need to take a bunch of photos. Sometimes, all you need is to press the shutter at the right time." I really admire his ability to create his work in different situations and places. As an artist myself, I am not used to this process and mindset; I am used to being able to create my work over time. After several expeditions with Ted, seeing him work has really helped me grow as an artist and as a person.

When Ted first asked me to join him on a trip to North Korea, I was extremely excited, because it had always been a dream of mine to see this mysterious country with my own eyes. Often, when traveling in other countries, we would spend most of our time wandering around the cities, exploring local markets and alleyways, and observing the mundane daily life of the locals. North Korea was a totally different experience. When we first got to Beijing before flying into North Korea, our agent explained the rules about going into the region—what to do and what not to do. He also mentioned the kindness of North Koreans, and said as long as we respected their culture, we would be fine. After arriving, we were accompanied by two tour guides at all times and were limited in what we were permitted to see. Most of the time, I was quite surprised that we were allowed to take photos and was extremely excited about the moments Ted was able to capture.

The scenery in North Korea was not exciting in comparison to other places, but being there was an experience like no other. Everything felt surreal when we first arrived. Time seemed to have frozen in the 1950s. Walking the streets, seeing the architecture, and noticing the way people dressed made us feel like we were on a movie set. As outsiders, we realized we would never know what people's lives were really like there, but things started making more sense after a day or two. People from the "outside world" usually portray North Koreans as strange, robot-like people, but that is not at all the case. One day, after visiting the International Friendship Museum, Ted asked if we could stop to check out a pavilion by a river. Our tour guide hesitated at first, but decided to stop the car and let us explore for a bit. We found a few middle-aged men relaxing on a bench next to the pavilion who waved and said hi to us as we were crossing the street toward them. We were very surprised because they were the first real local people who talked to us, proactively. One excitedly exclaimed, "Our country so beautiful!" and we all laughed together. Yes, it is so beautiful! Because there are people in it just like you and me. Most people in North Korea are honest souls who work hard to earn what they have. Their predicament is not their fault. They do not know any better. It is the system that they are born into that has created a cage around them, around their thoughts, and around their imaginations.

One day, Ted was shooting three people throwing blankets on a rooftop from a hill. While waiting, one of our tour guides, Ri, asked me what was so great about the scene. I told him that the composition and color of the scene was really joyful, and Ted was trying to make it work. Ri asked to see what Ted had shot and said, "It's not pretty." It's an understandable reaction once you become aware that most of the artwork in North Korea consists of paintings featuring either mountains, oceans, animals, portraits, or propaganda. Any photographs that we saw were mostly images of leaders, or family photos. North Koreans are not exposed to a diverse body of art. The result is that their idea of art and beauty is somewhat limited.

Our guide Ri was a smart and driven person with a great personality, who also spoke perfect Mandarin and English. He would chat with us, make jokes, and answer every random question we threw at him. While sharing his life story, he told us he used to work abroad in China doing government business. I asked him, since he had been abroad, what his thoughts were toward the outside world. He said, with reservation, "It is very different." I saw the hesitation in his eyes and did not want to push him, since I know it is a very sensitive subject. But unlike most North Koreans, including the men we'd met at the pavilion, Ri had seen another place and I continue to wonder, to this day, how it changed his point of view toward his own country.

On our way to the airport, Ri asked to look through Ted's camera. He asked Ted to delete a photo of a man riding his bike with a huge sack of crops. When I asked him why, Ri told us, "I understand that this is a nice photo to you, but he was not in his best outfit, looking his best, so it is considered a 'bad image' of our country." For someone only in North Korea for a brief time, some of these images may simply appear to show what the day-to-day lives of North Koreans are, and how normal everything is, even when compared to other cultures. However, the system there only allows for sanctioned images projected outwards to show what a proud nation it is.

North Korea is a unique place with a great people that we outsiders will never be able to see and comprehend fully. But seeing the beautiful moments that Ted has captured will give you a glimpse into what it is like in this often-misunderstood country.

— Yu-Ting Cheng

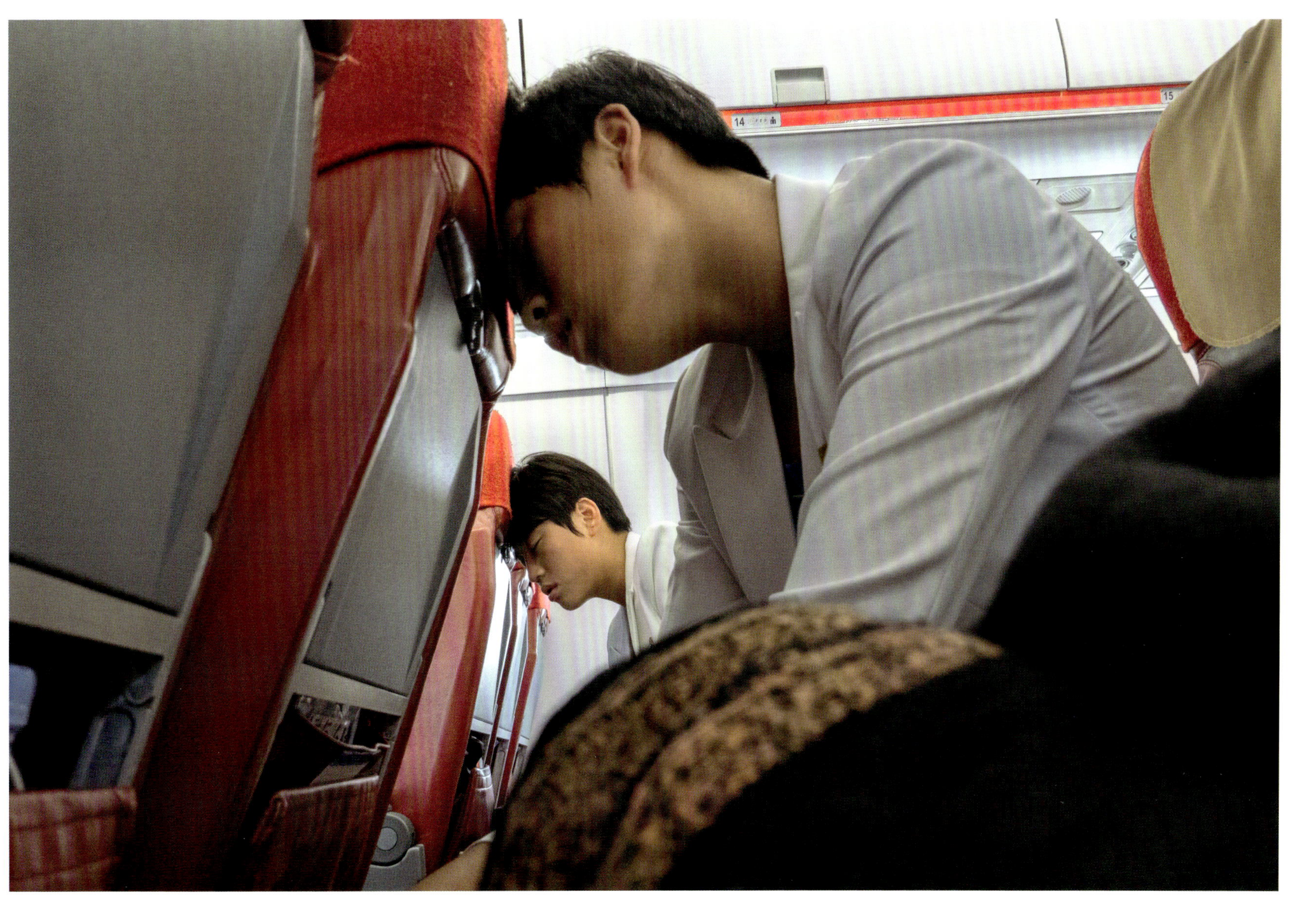

14
15

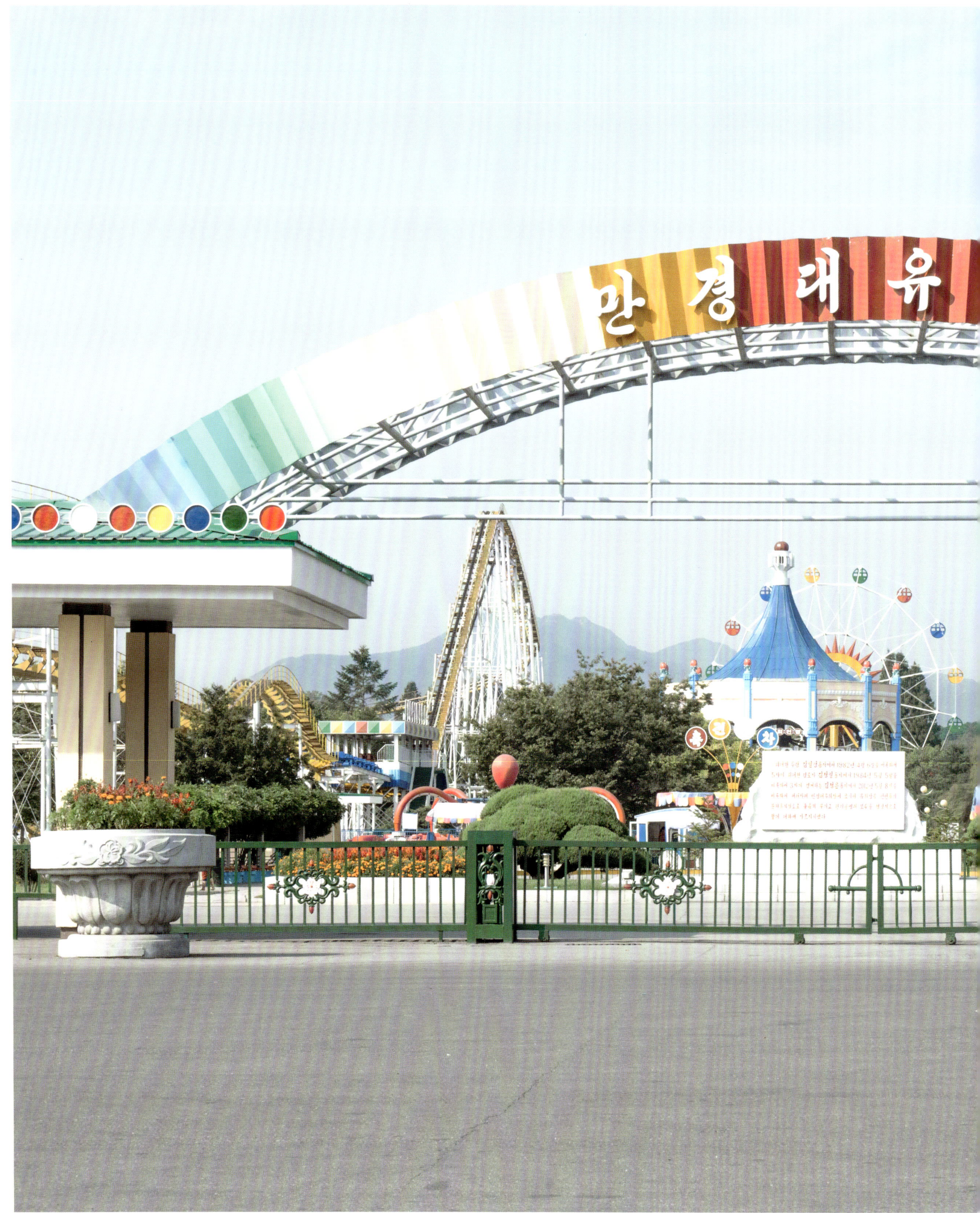

만 경 대 유

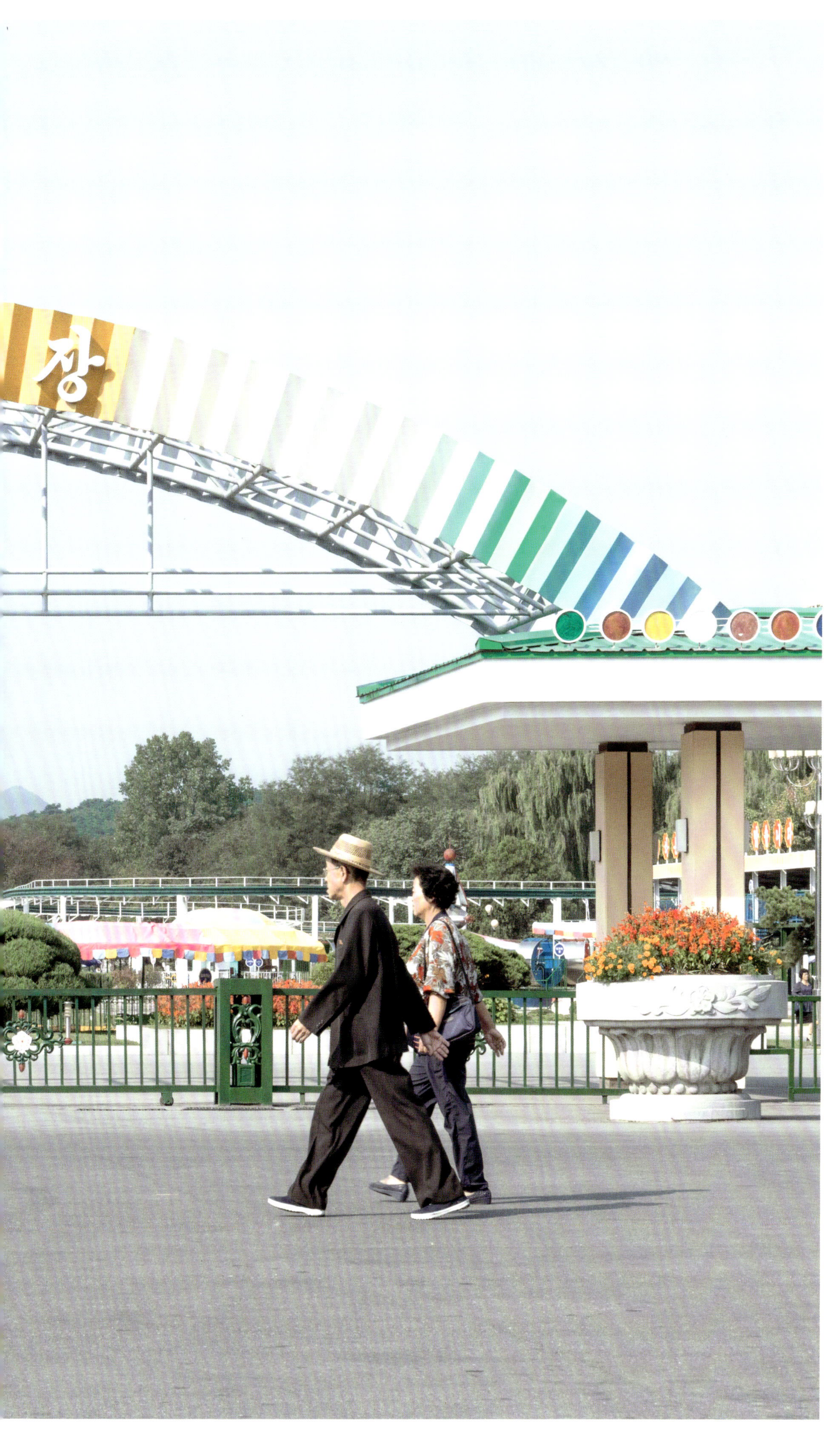
장

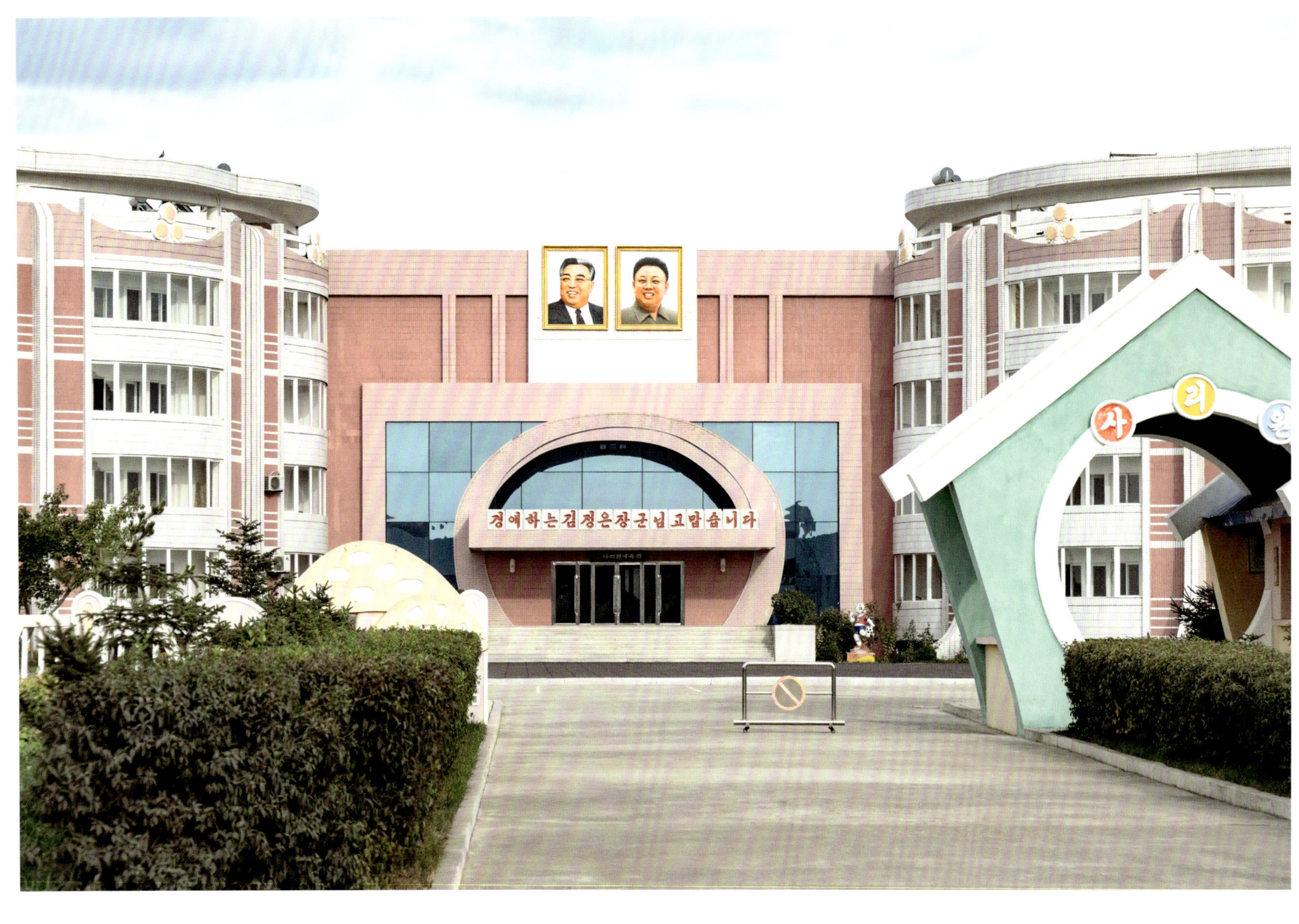

경애하는 김정은장군님 고맙습니다

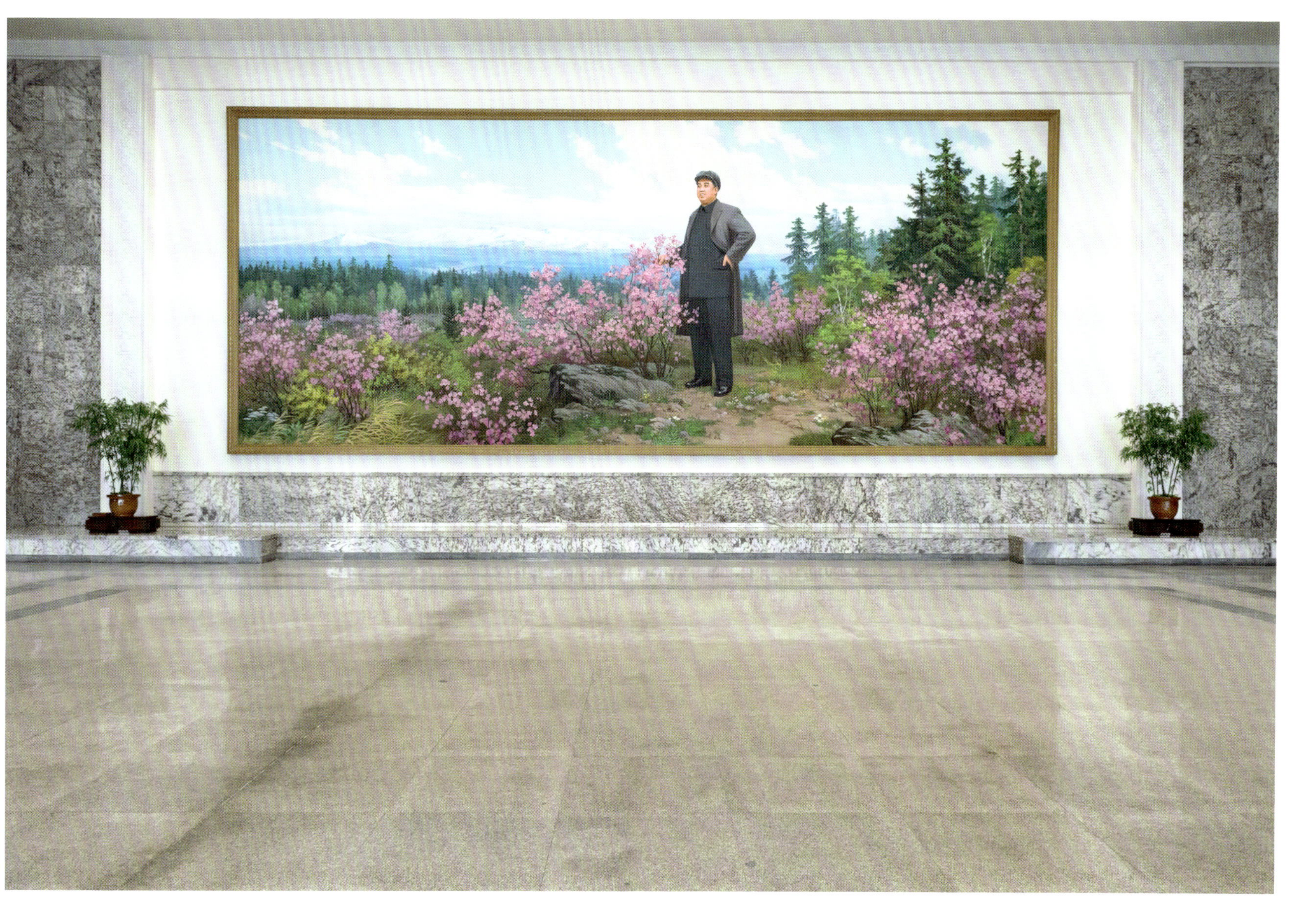

Like the dazzling
sunlight, enlightening us,

He is always in
our mind,

Our heart is like springtime.

Dear Supreme Leader,
Our Dear Supreme Leader,

He is our friendly Father!

It feels good to be in his protection.

His sunlight is the brightest.

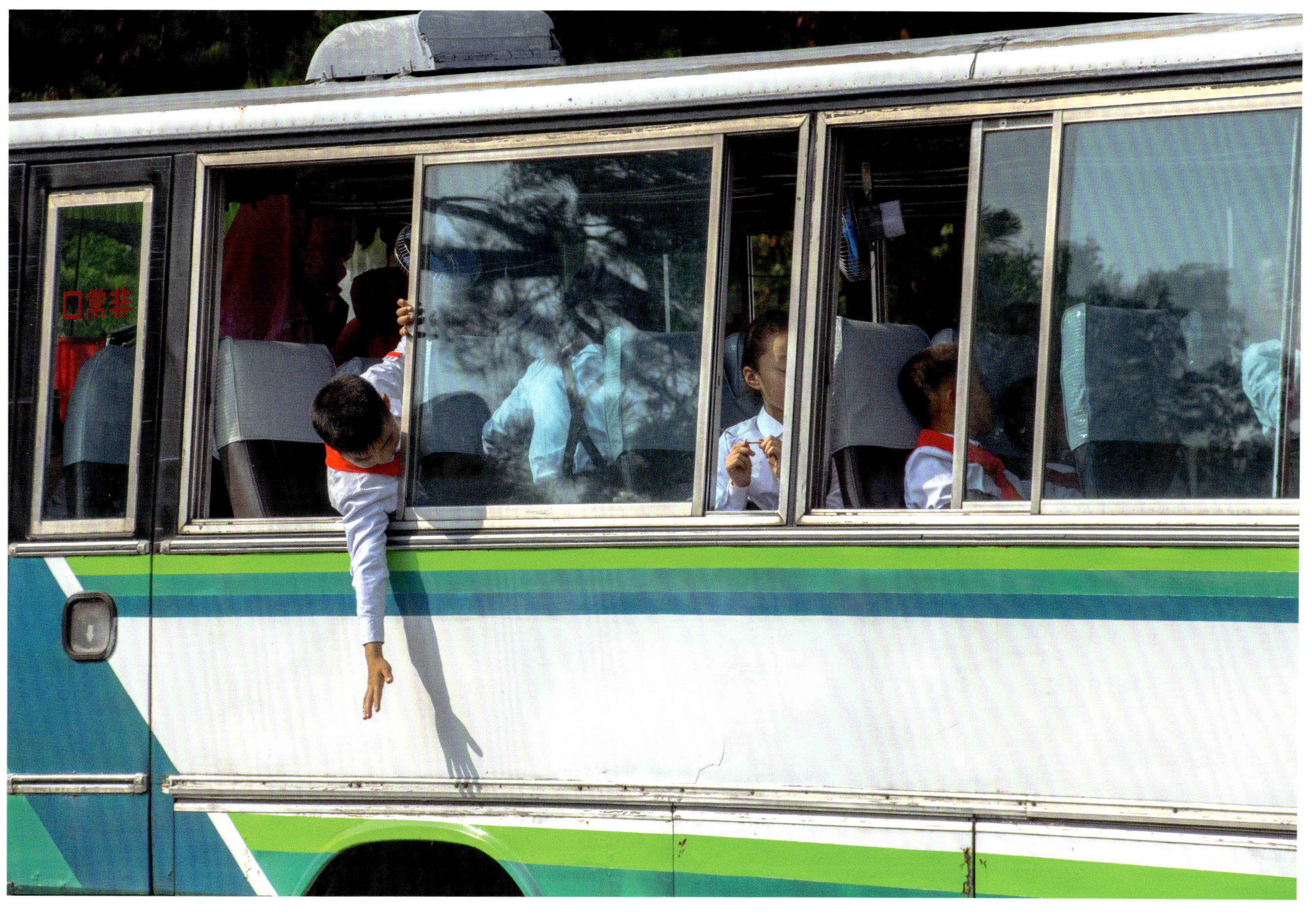

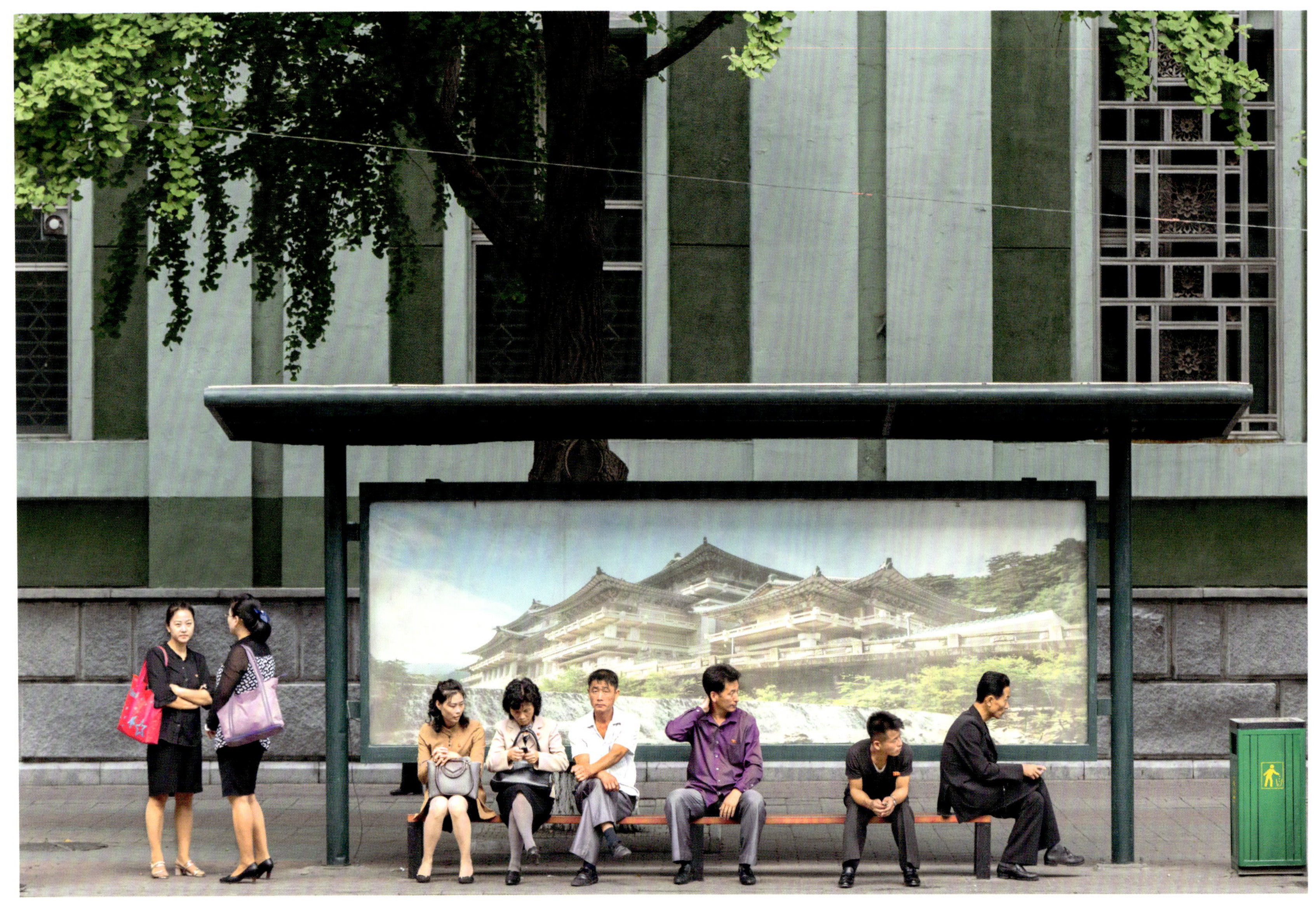

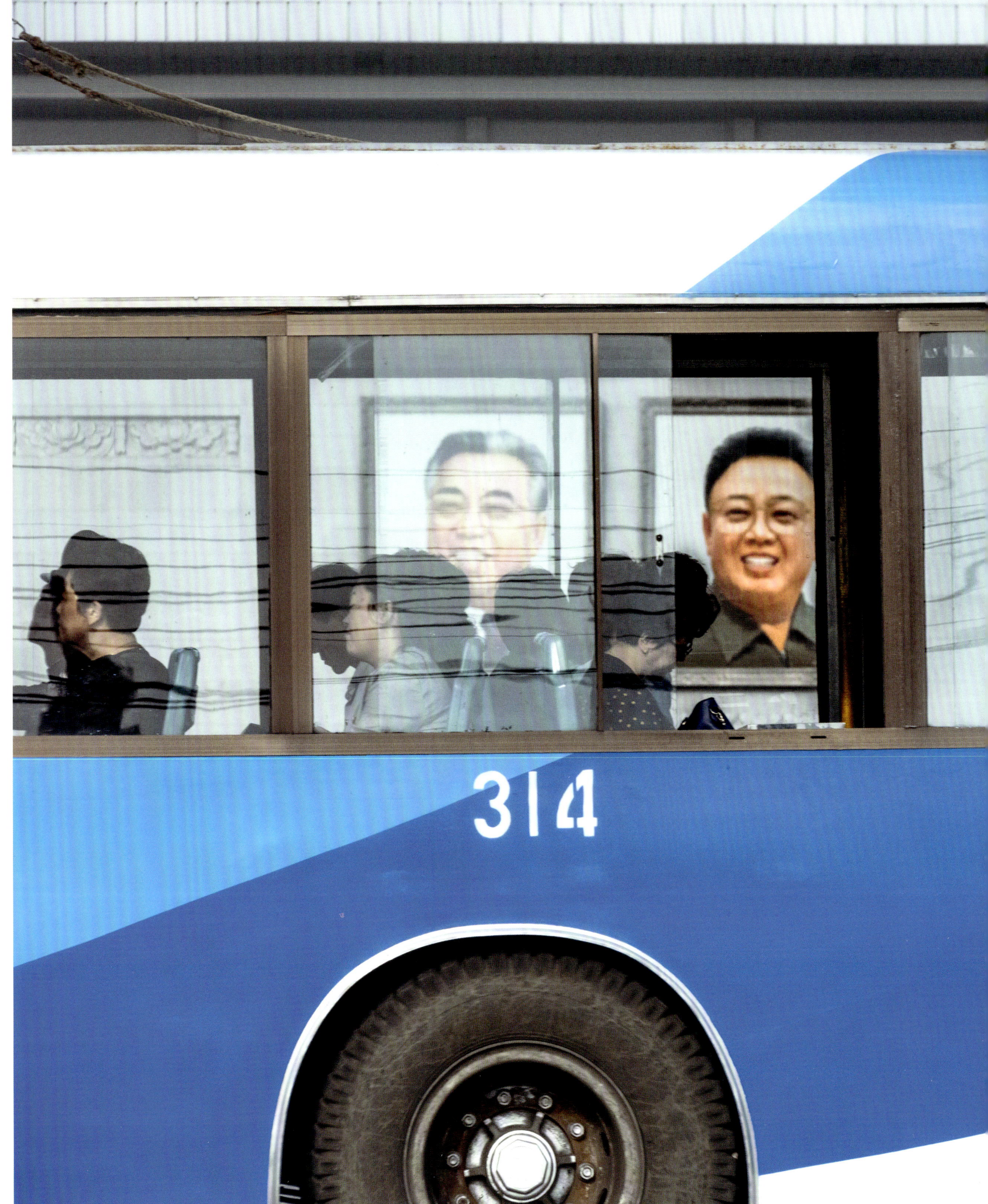

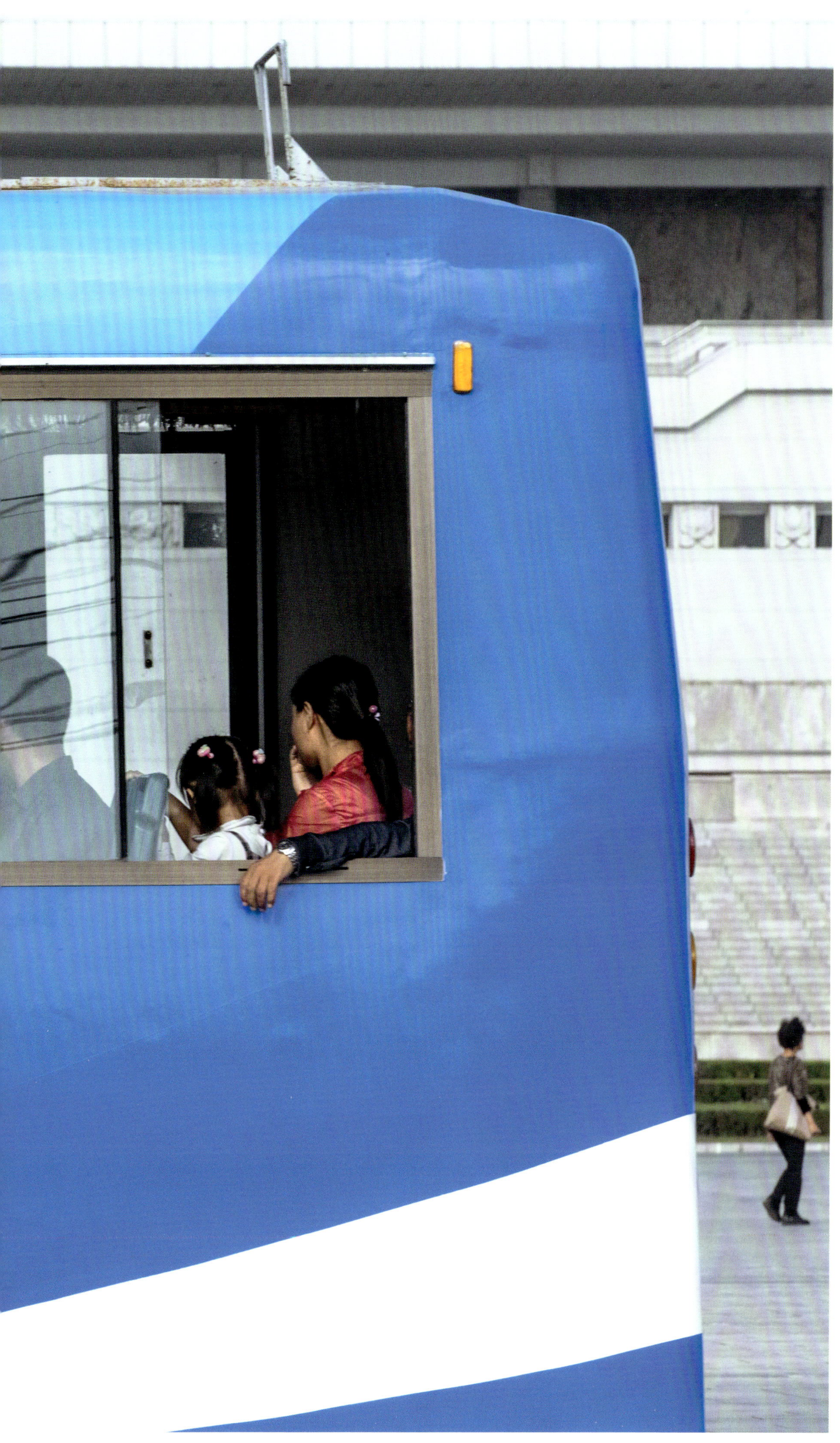

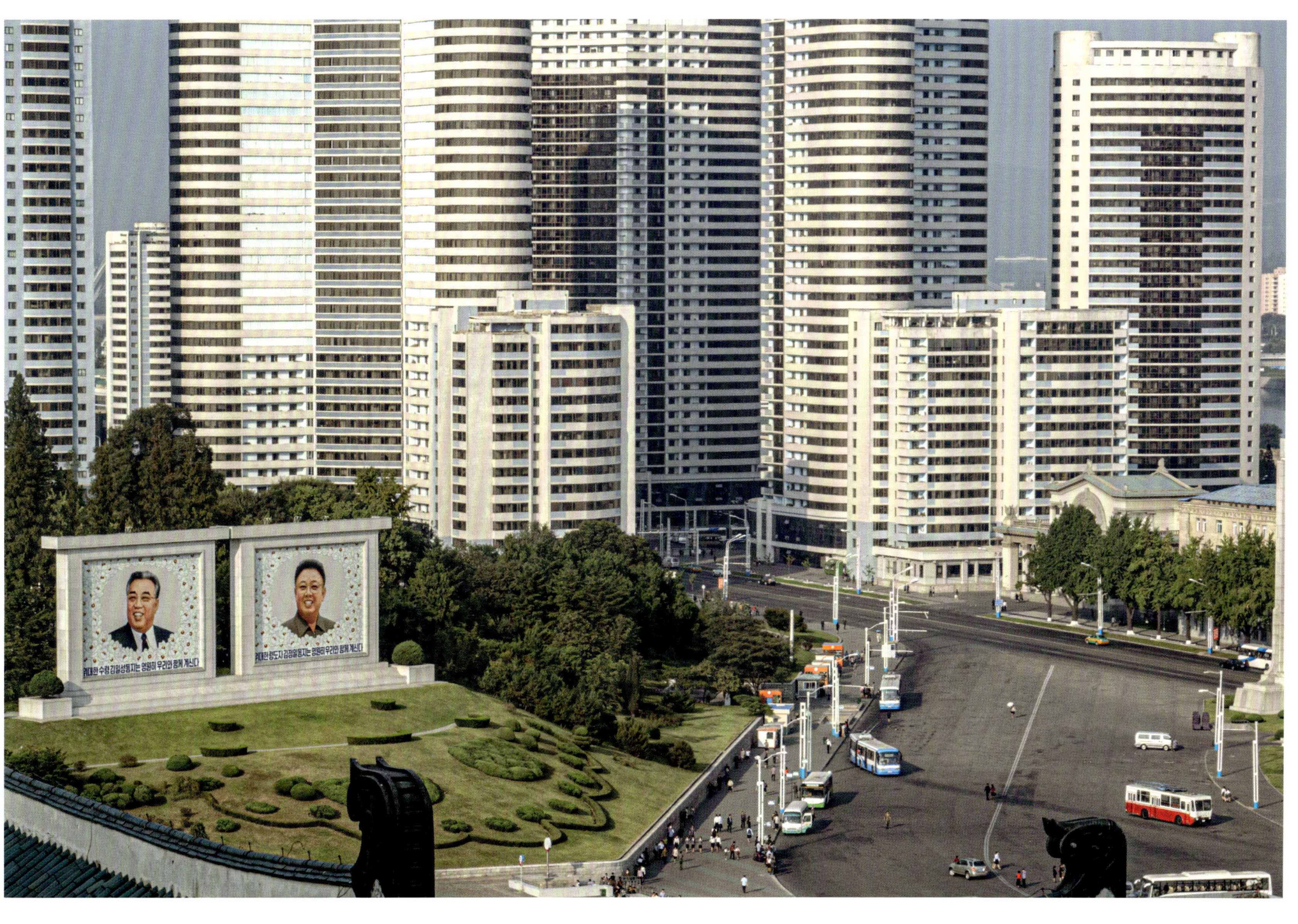

The will and affection of the general

They are the breath of my life

They are my only wish

They are my only wish

—from "Glorious and Admirable" (매혹과 흠모)
by The Moranbong Band

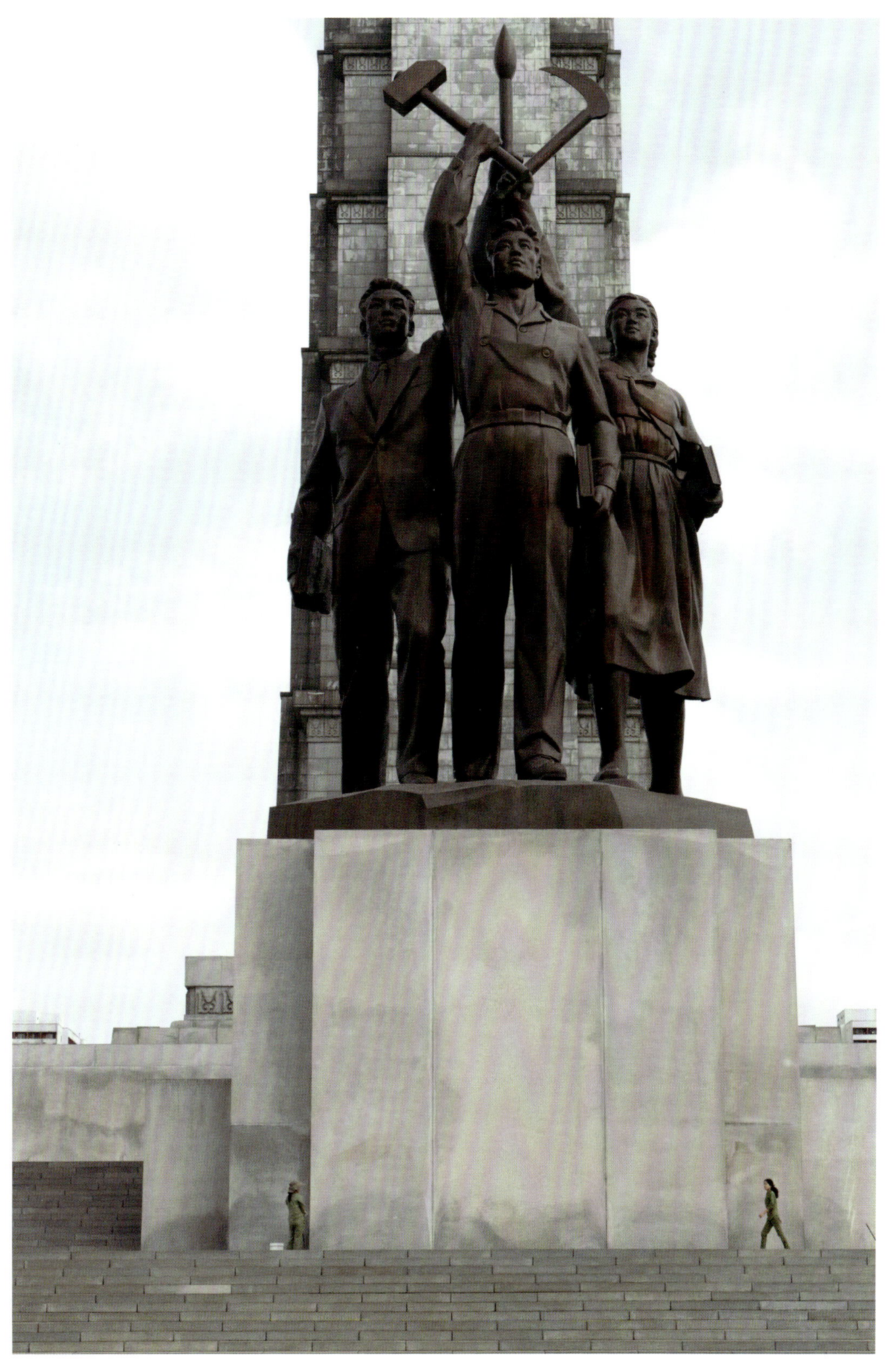

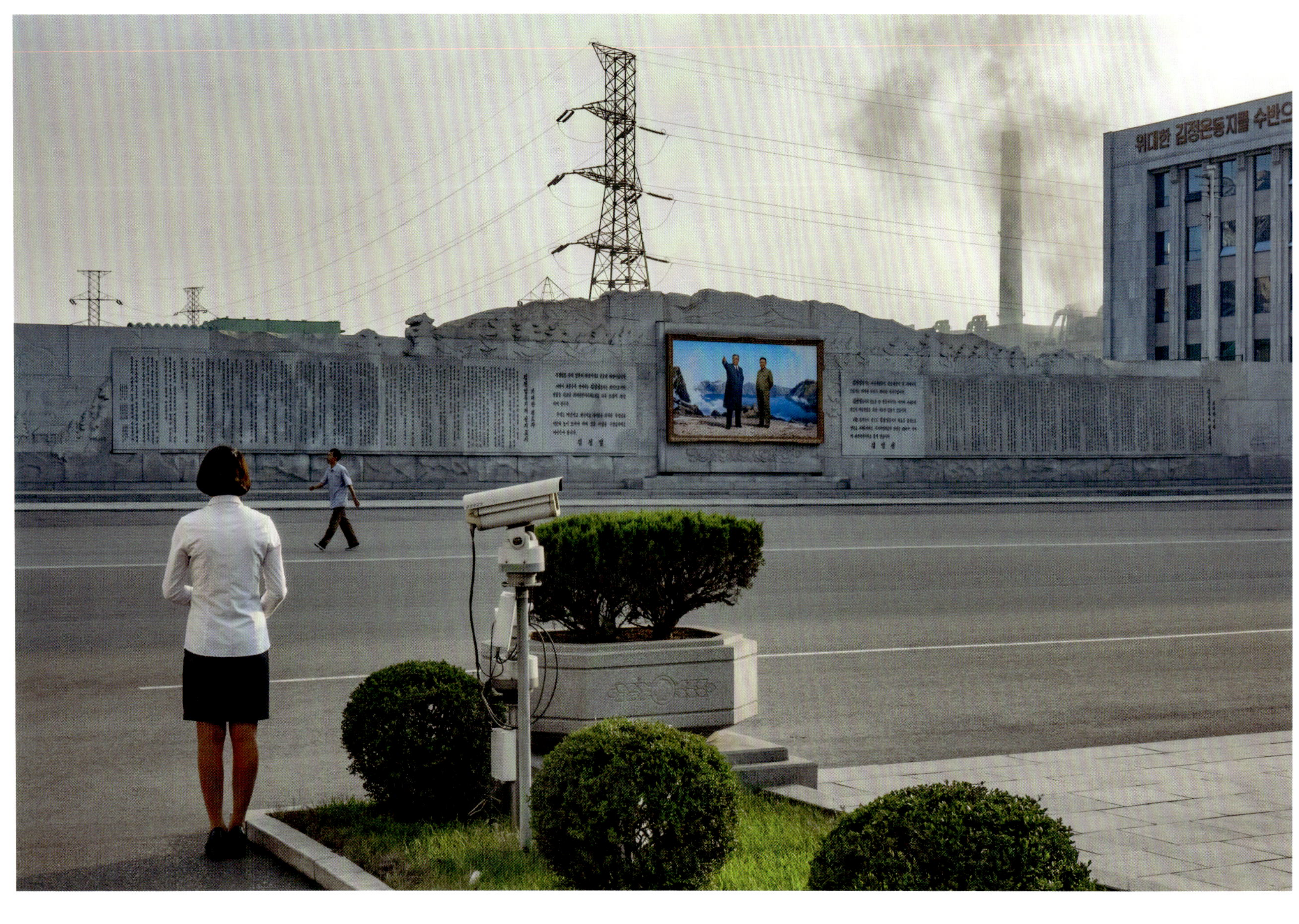

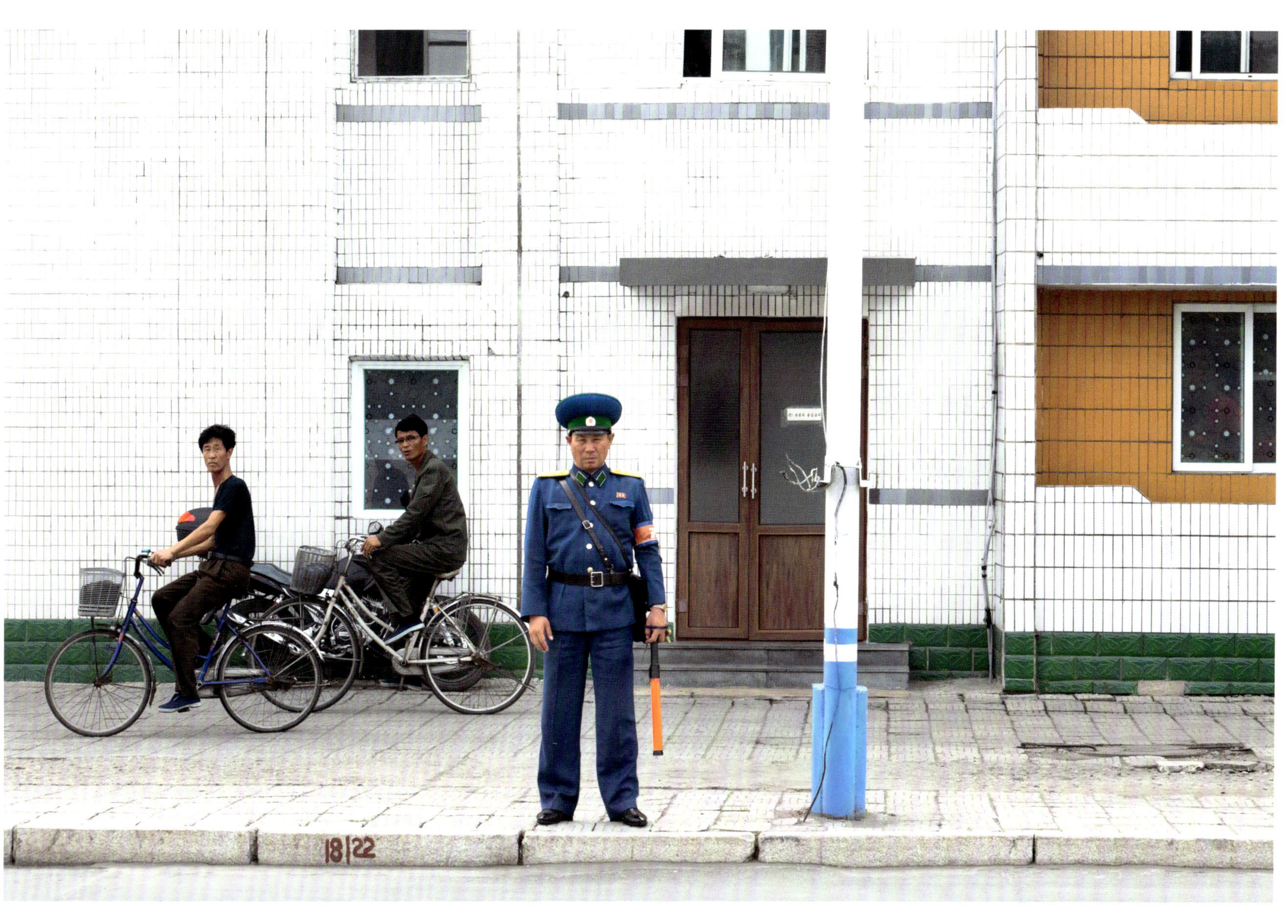

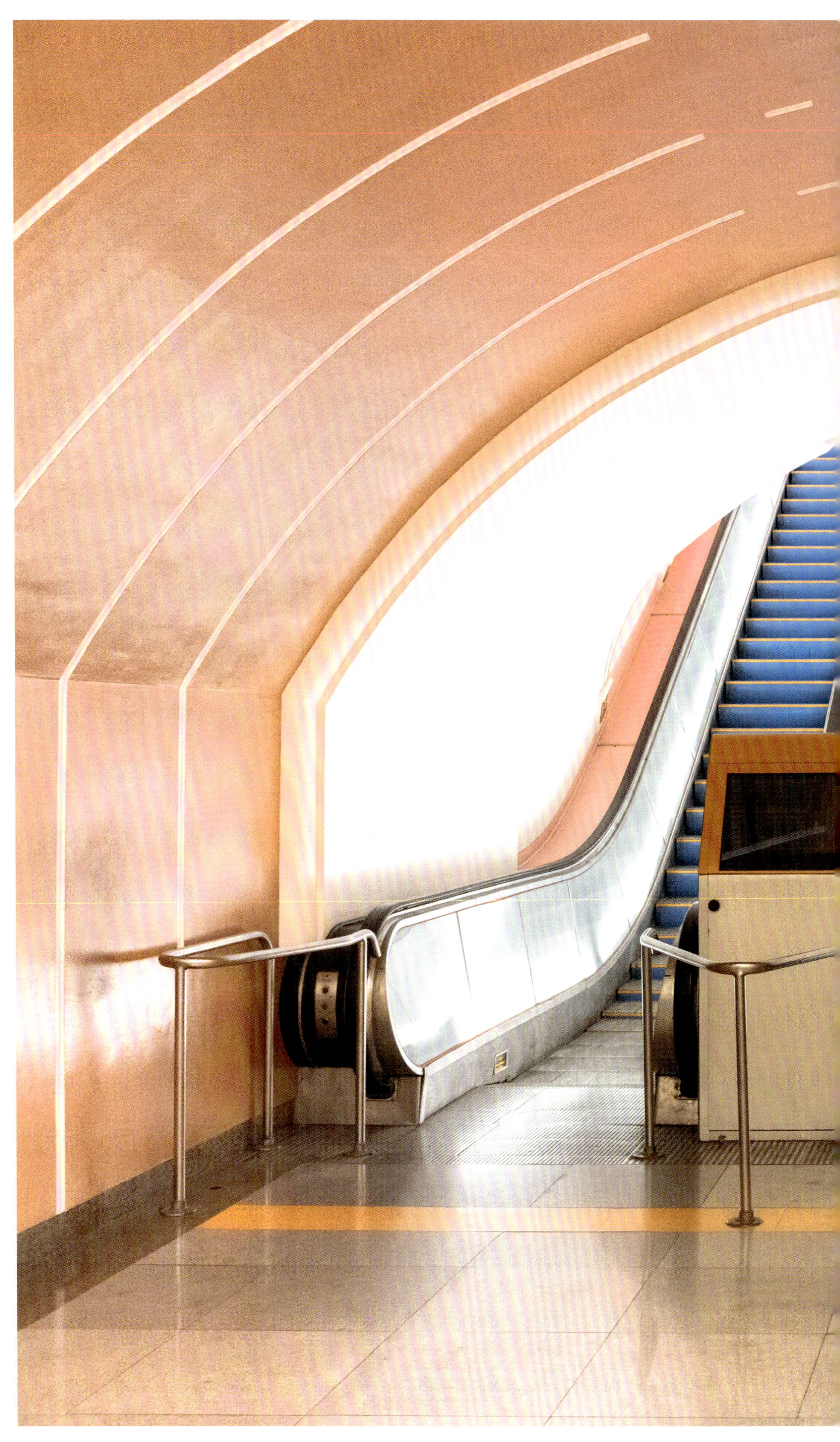

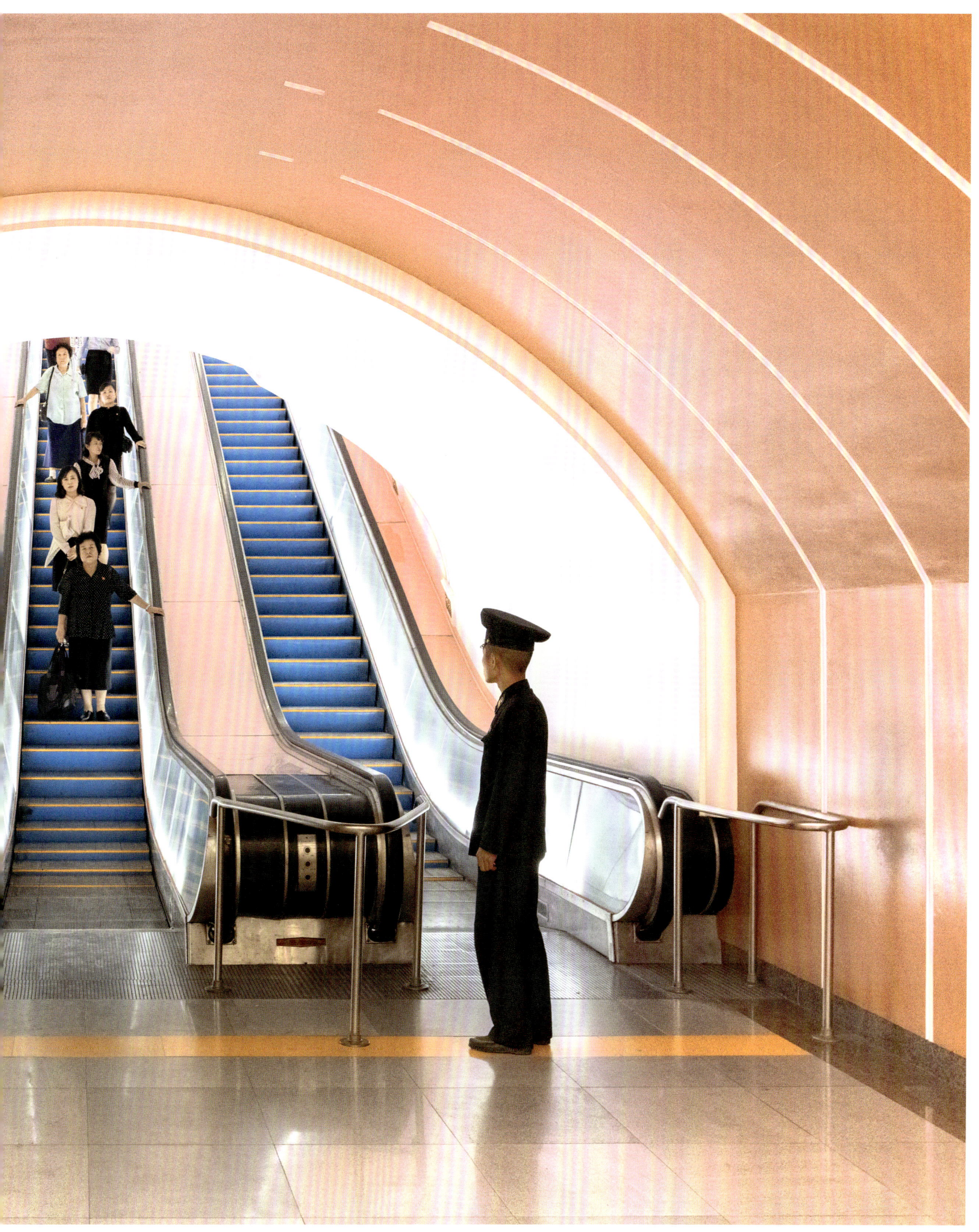

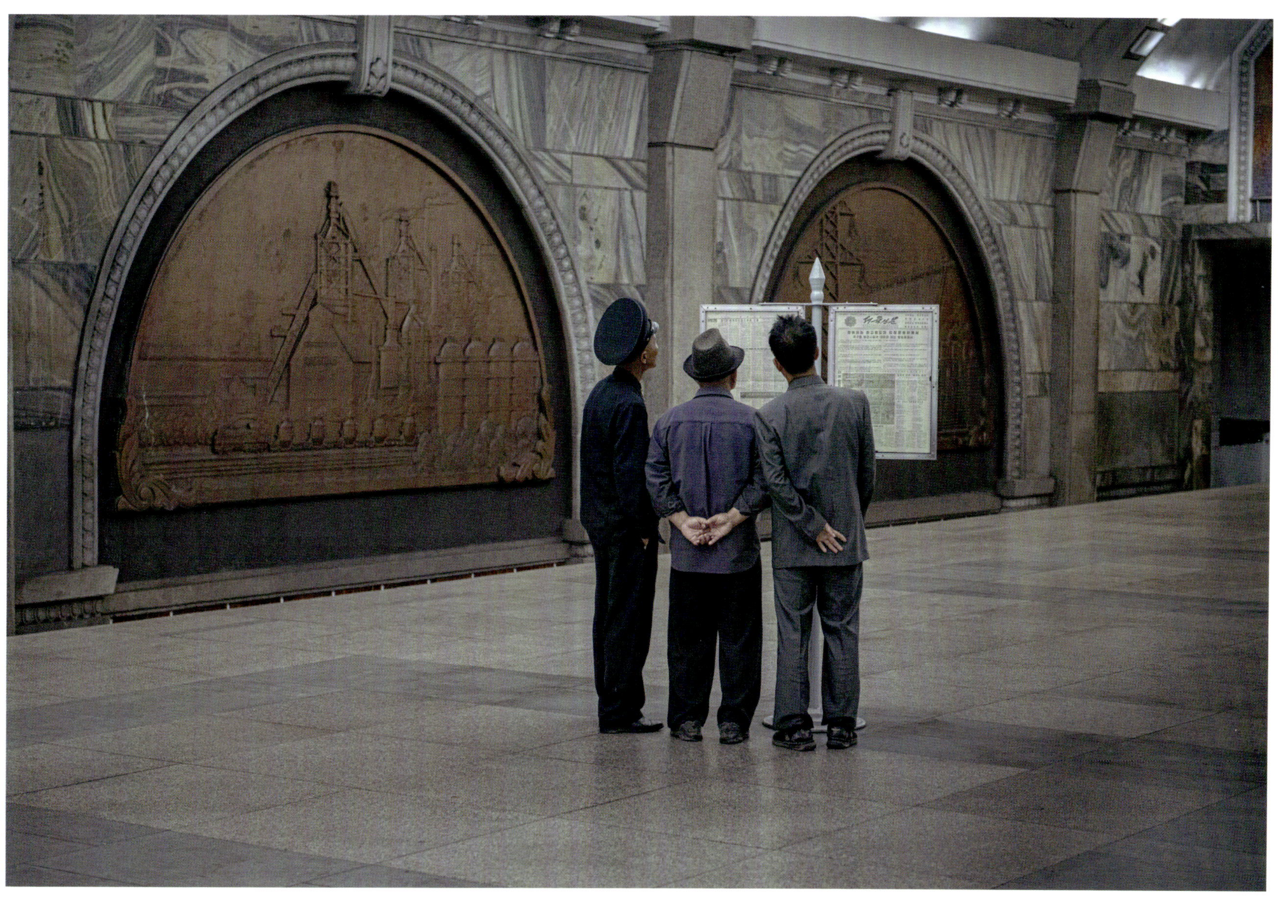

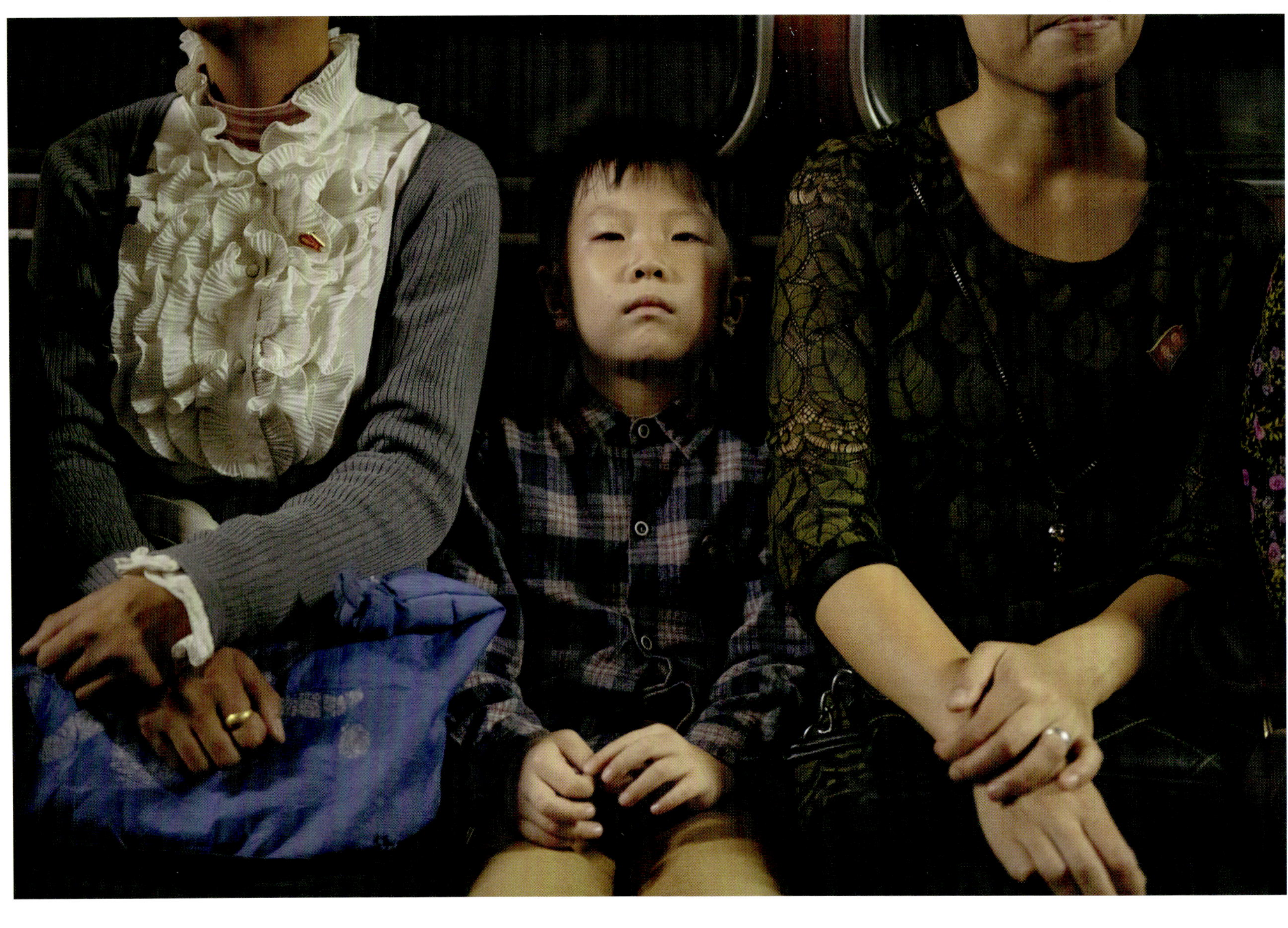

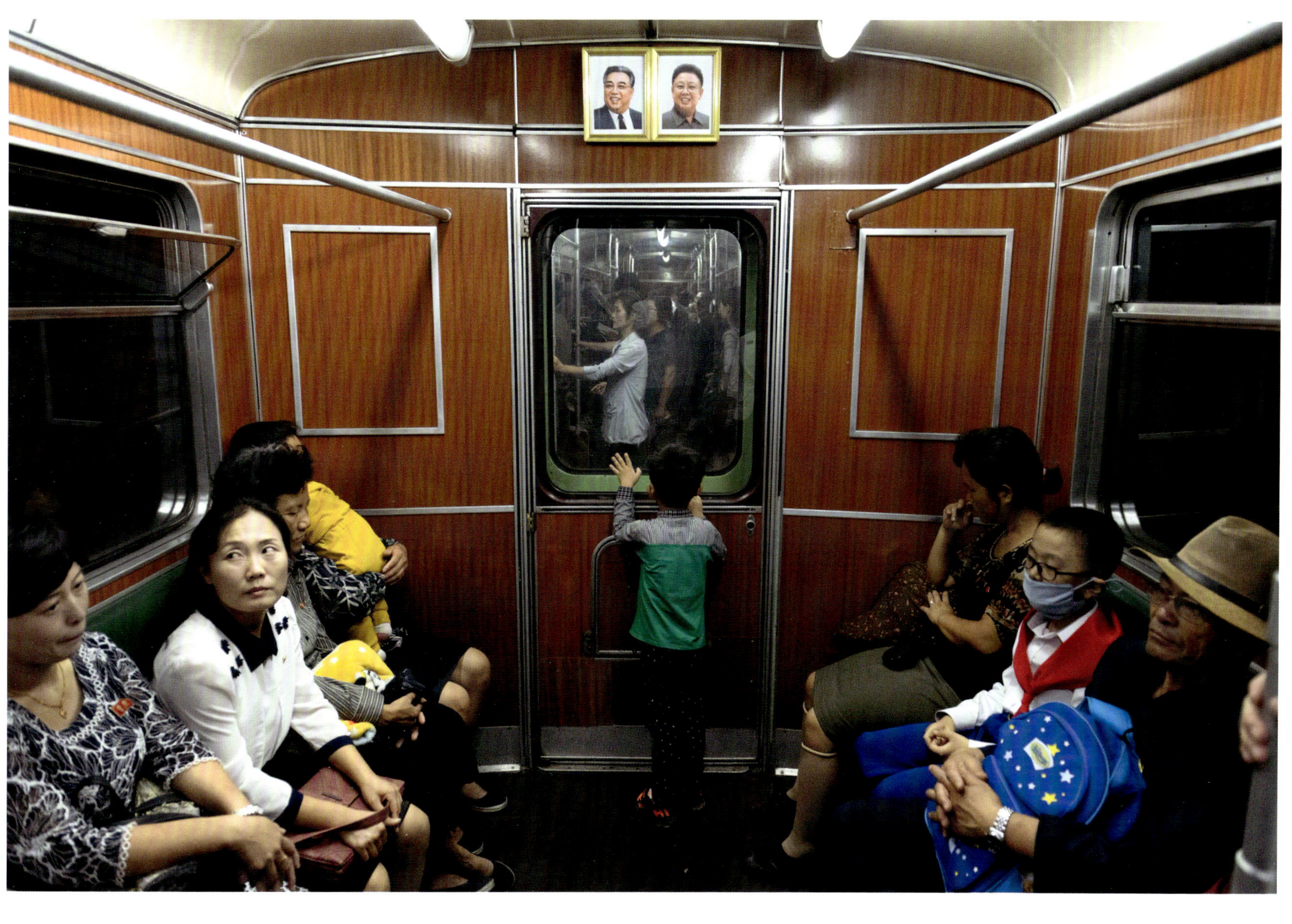

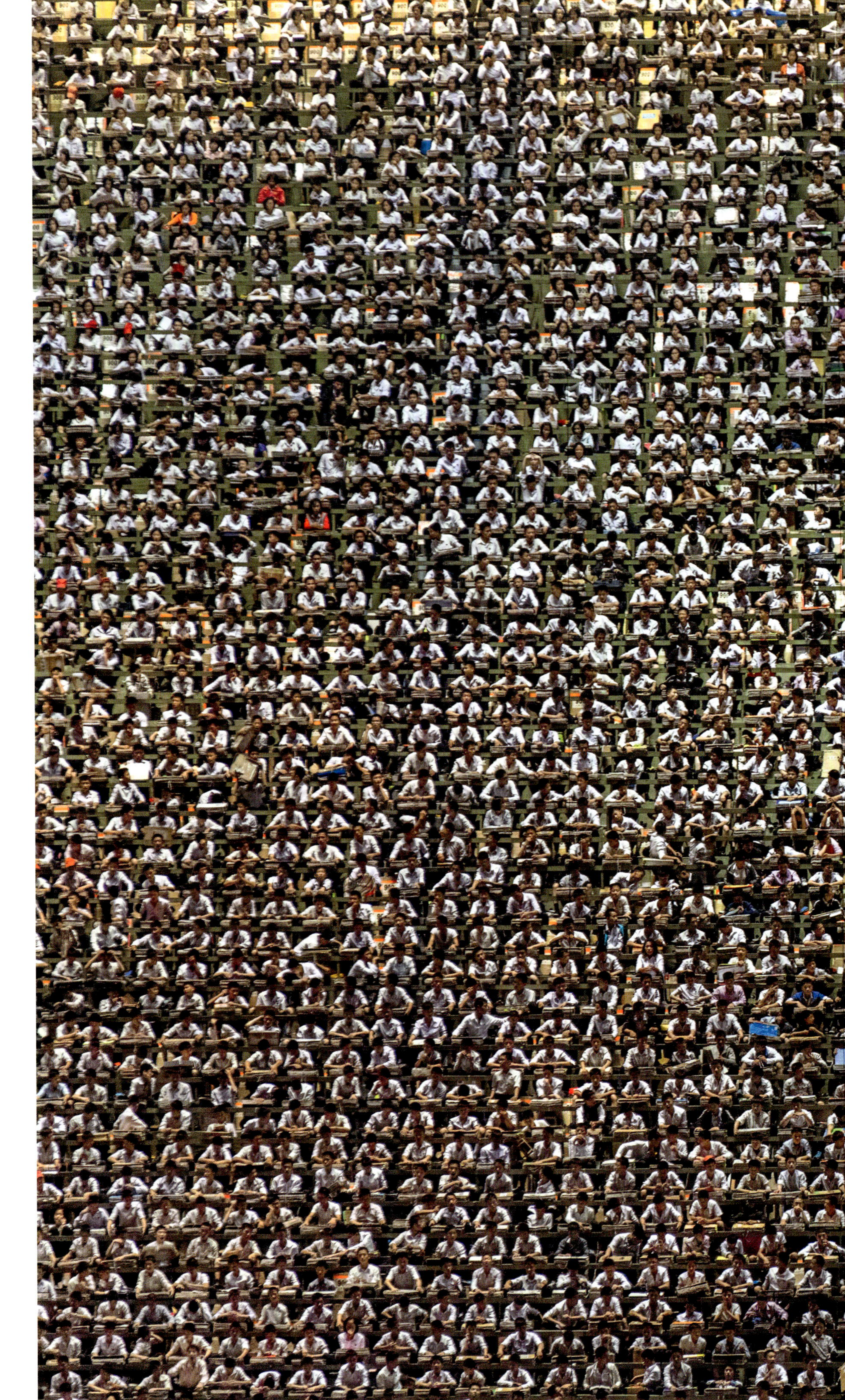

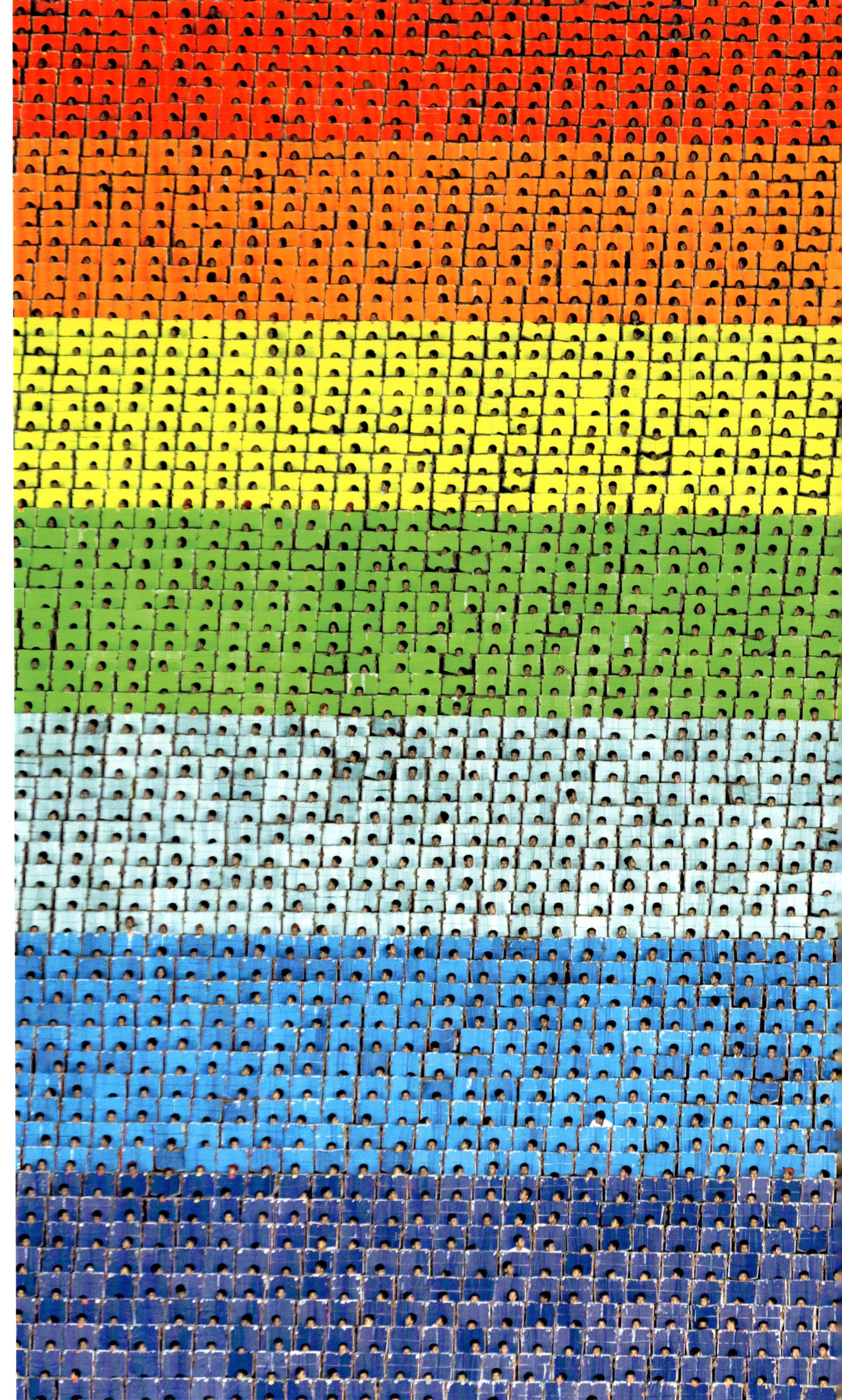

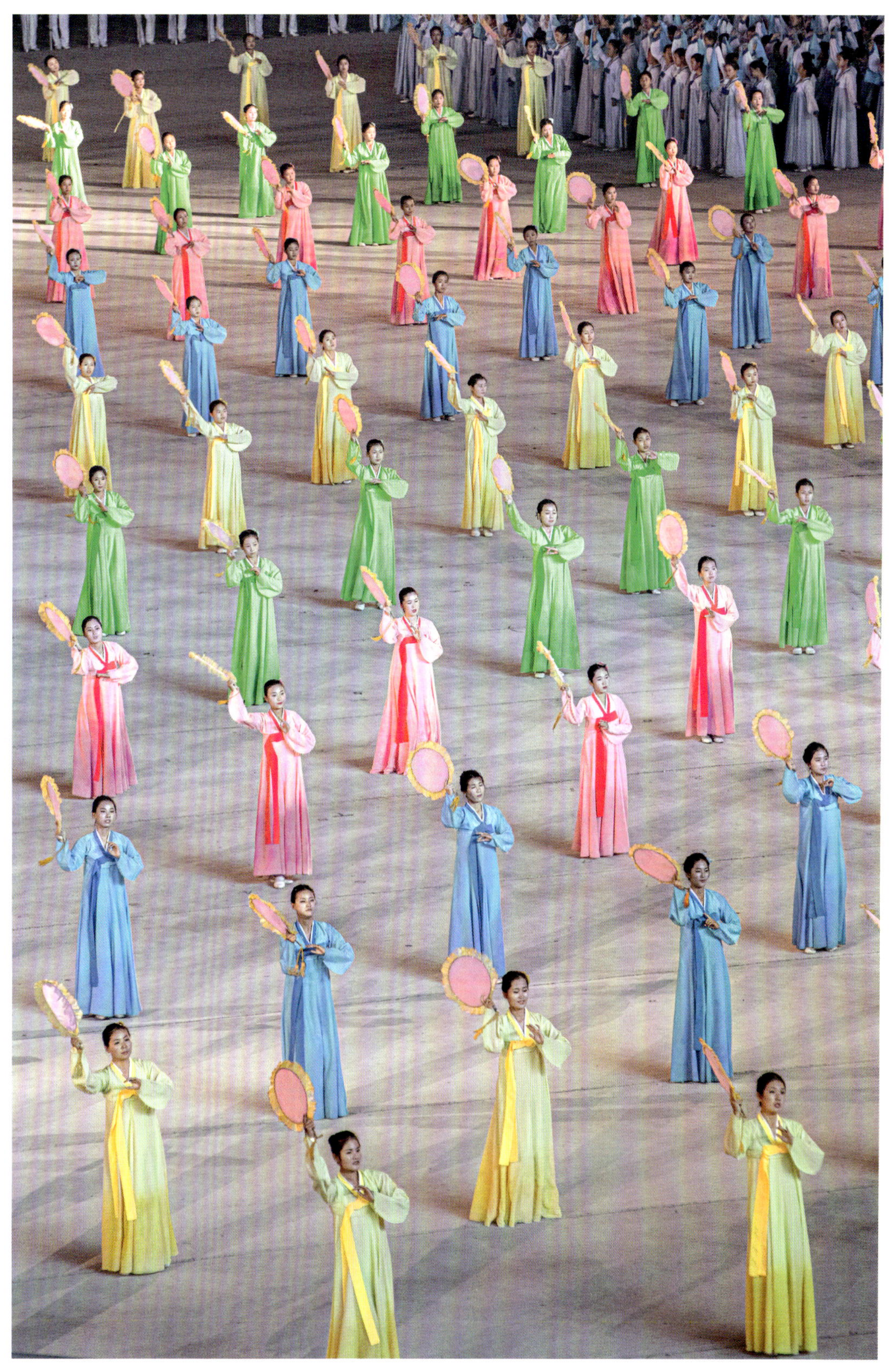

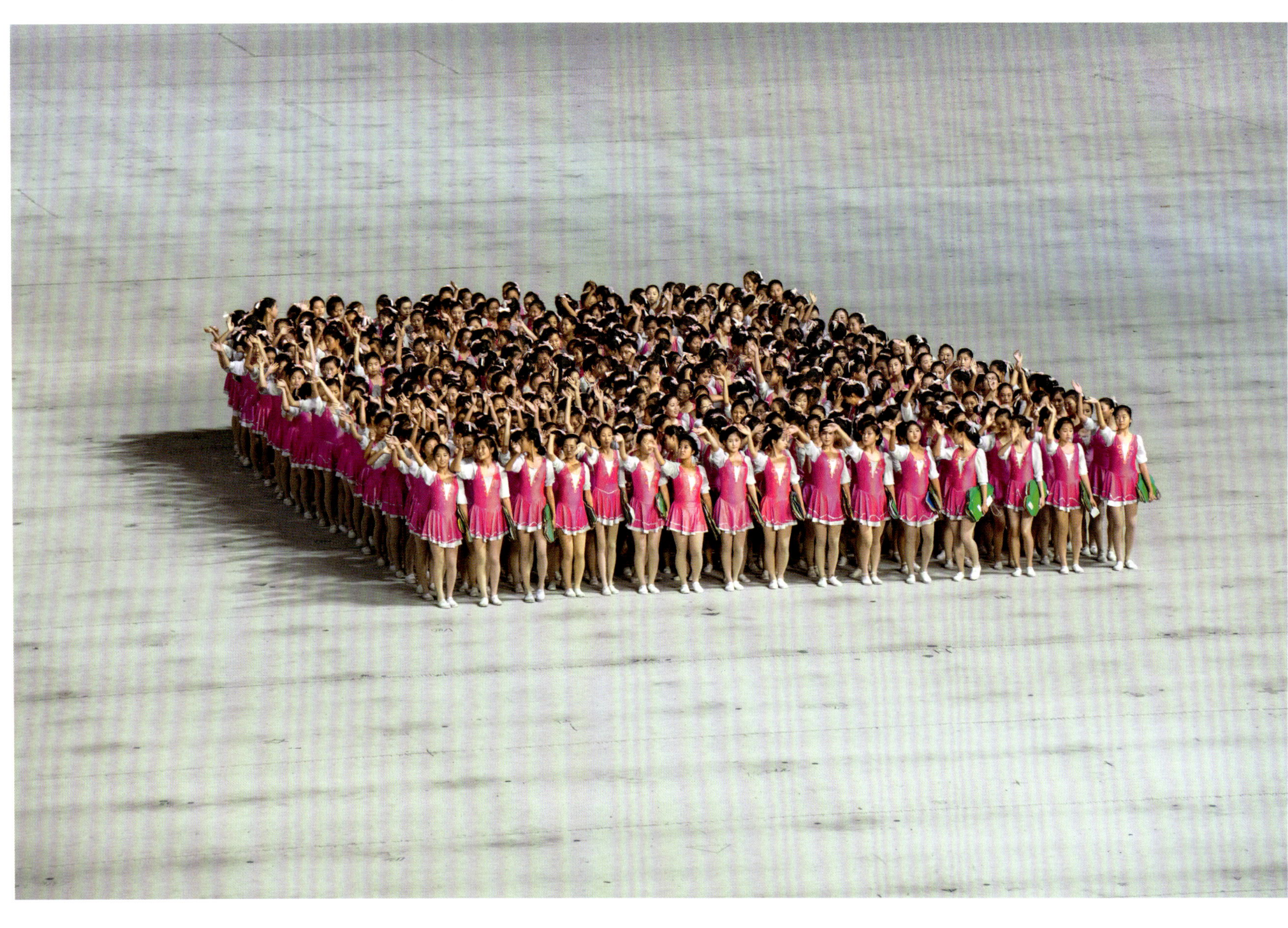

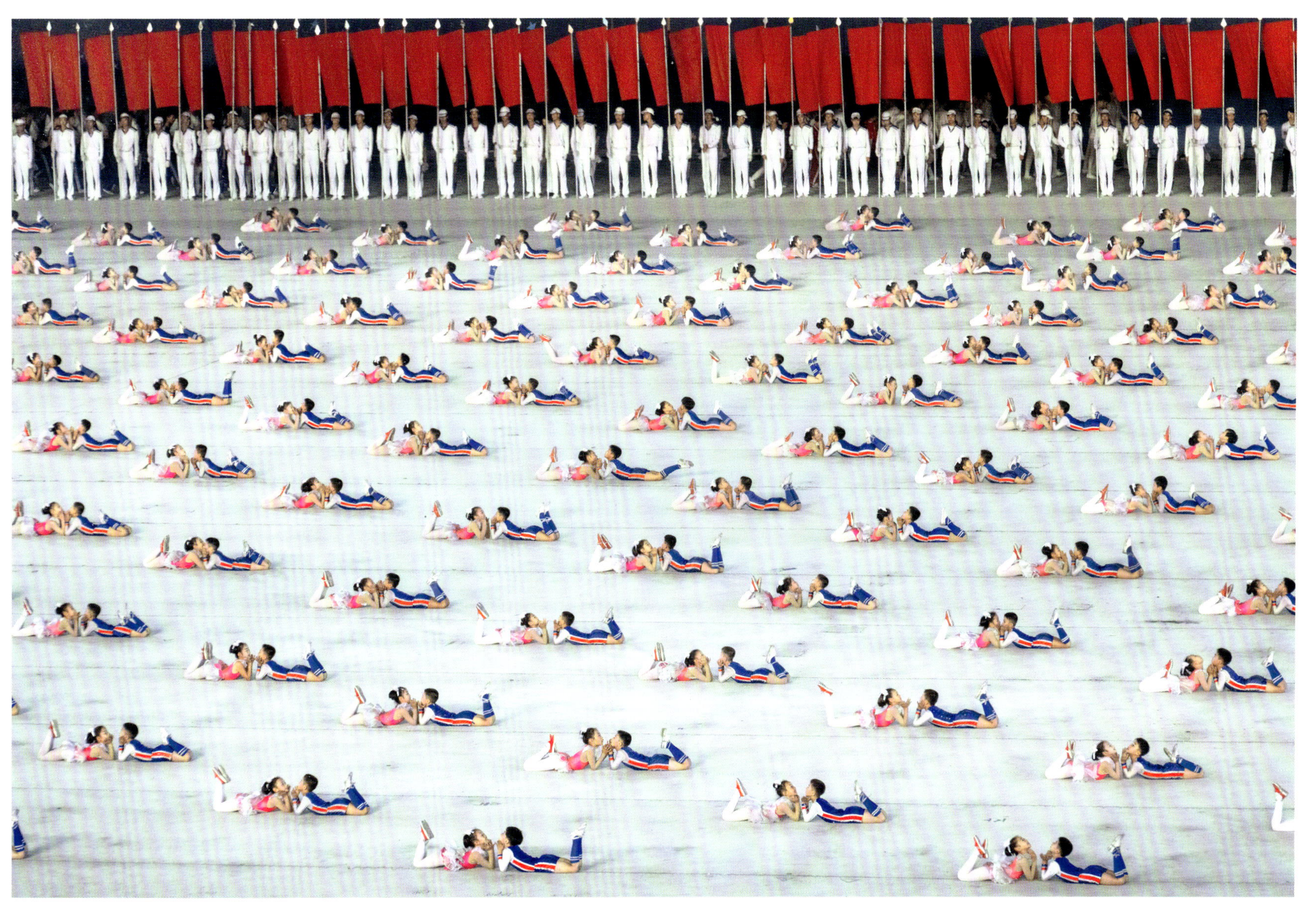

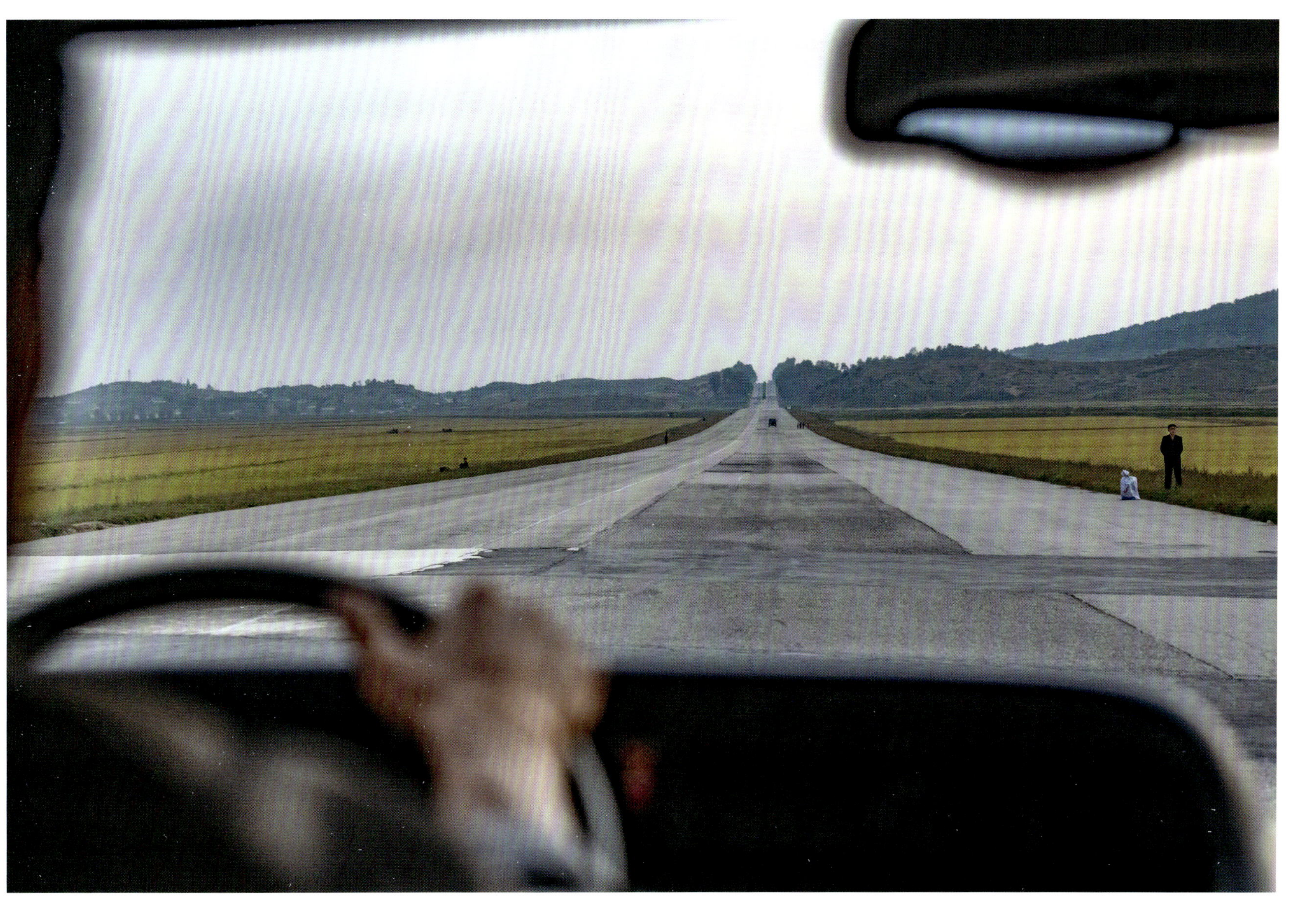

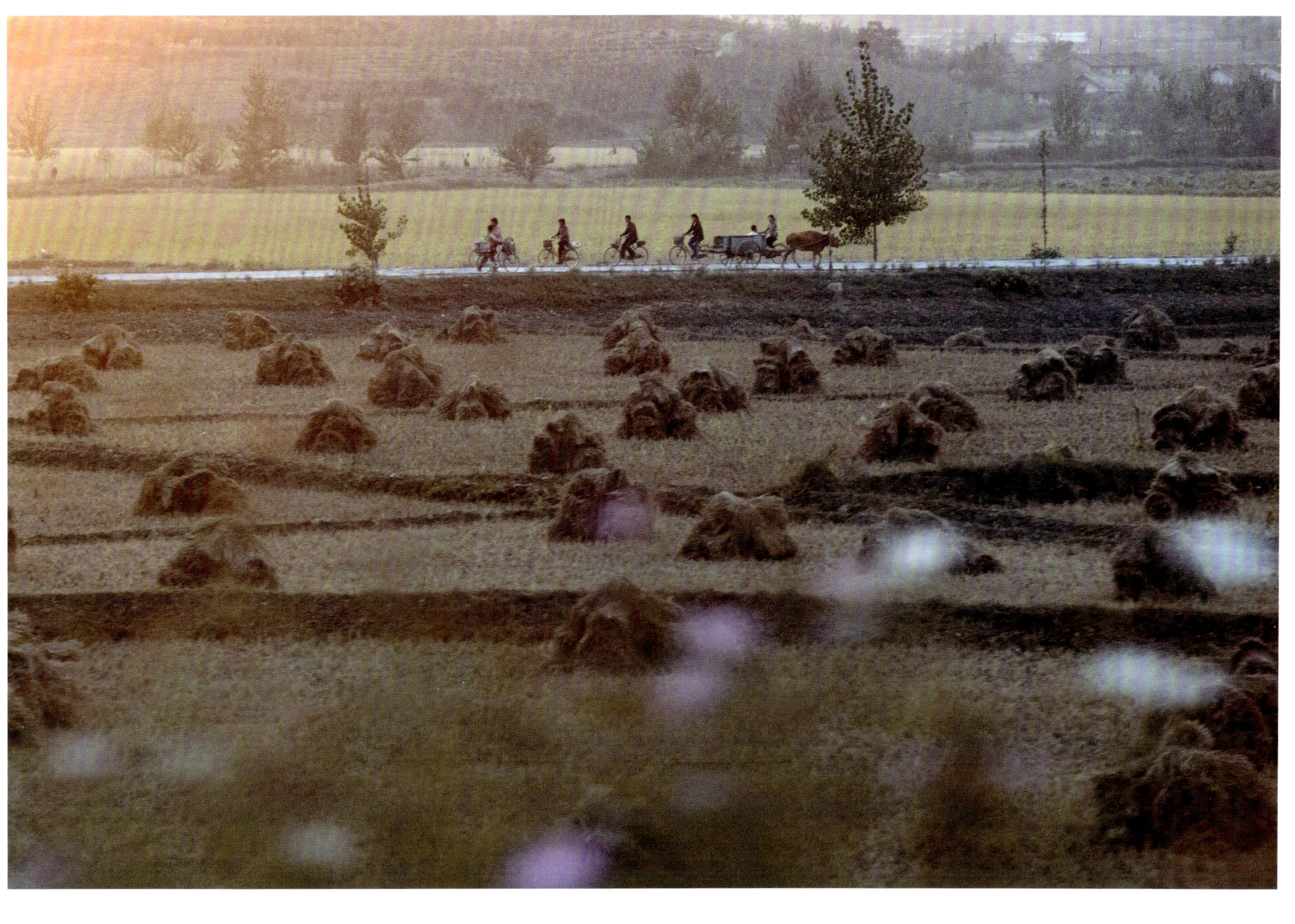

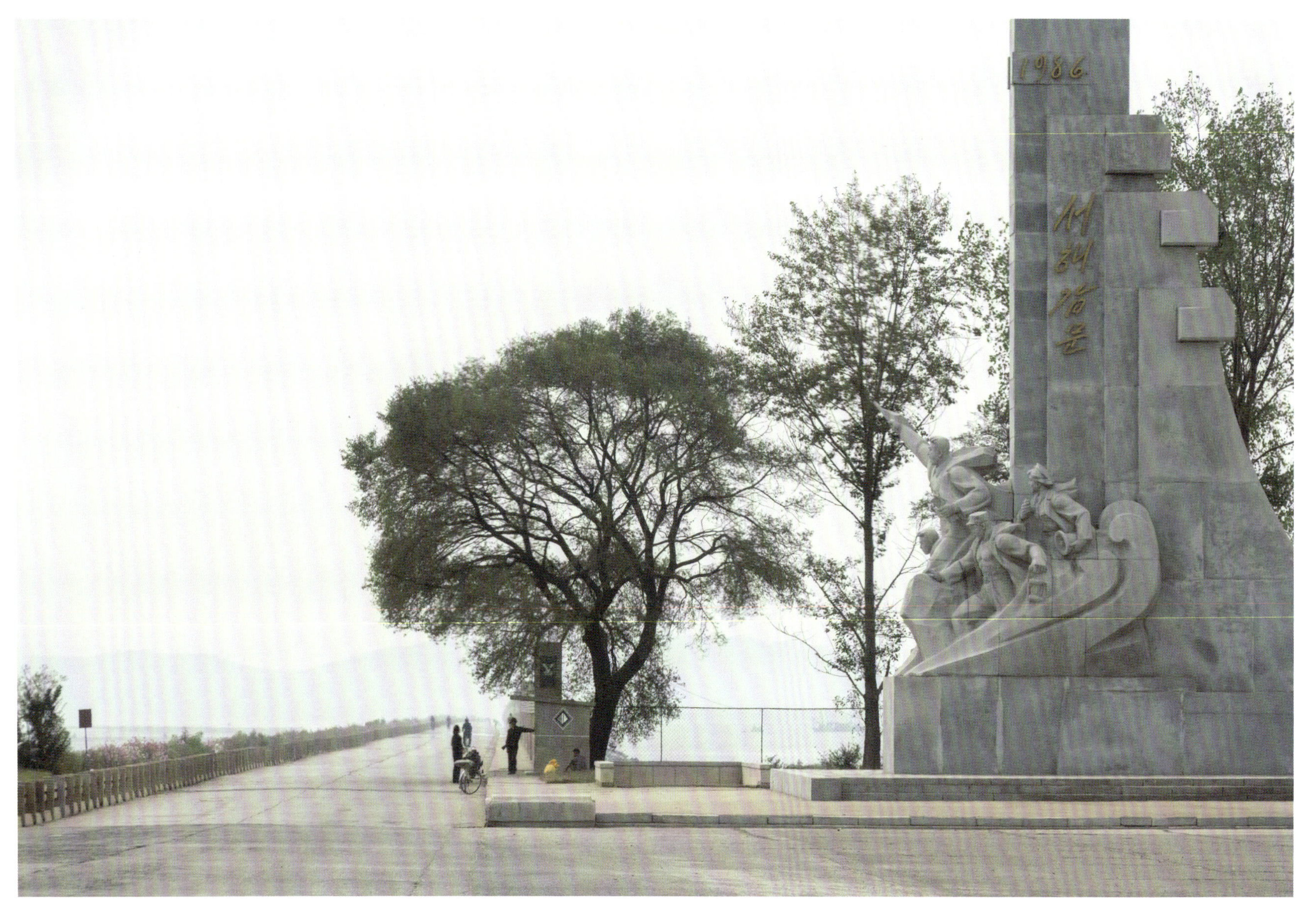

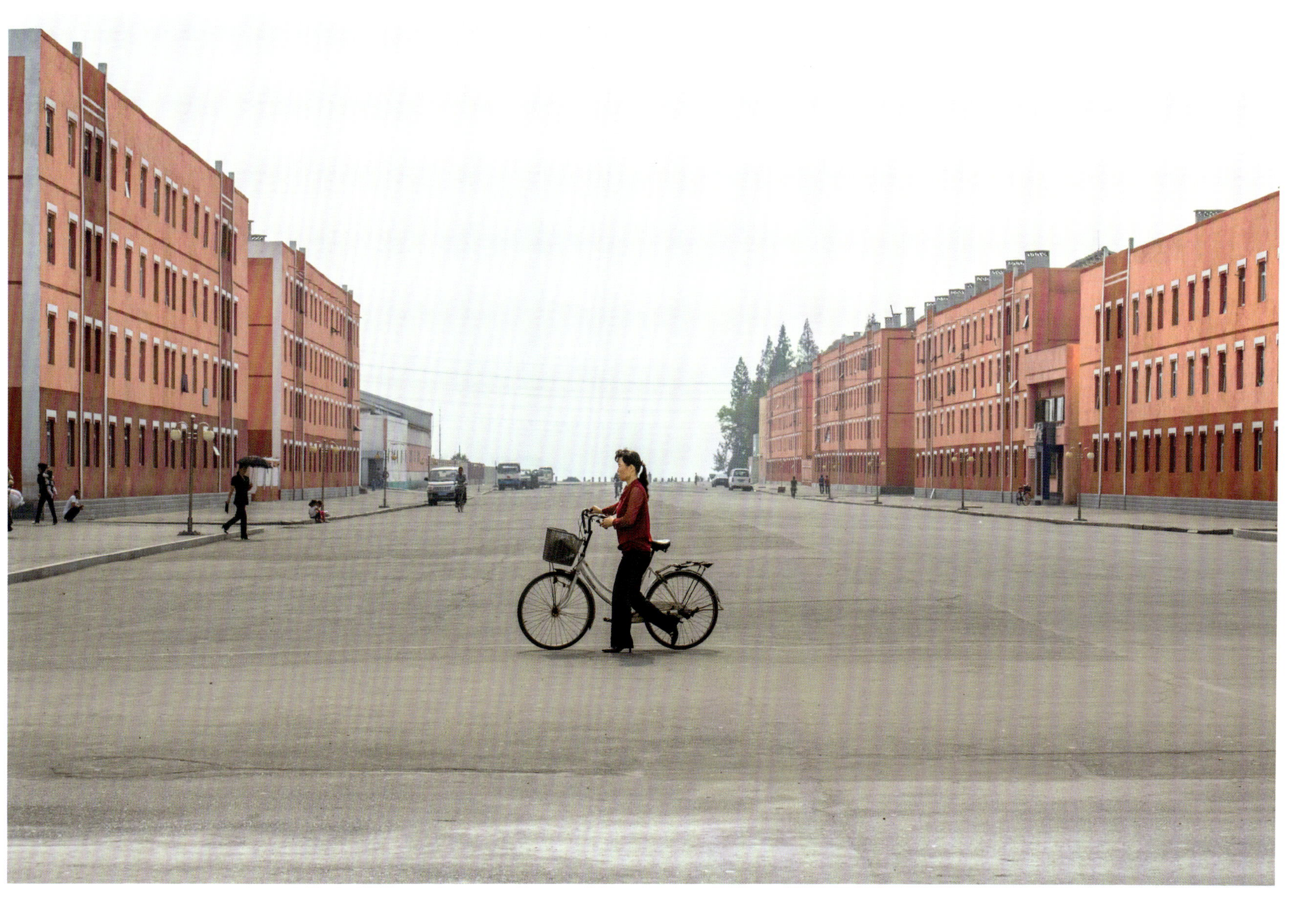

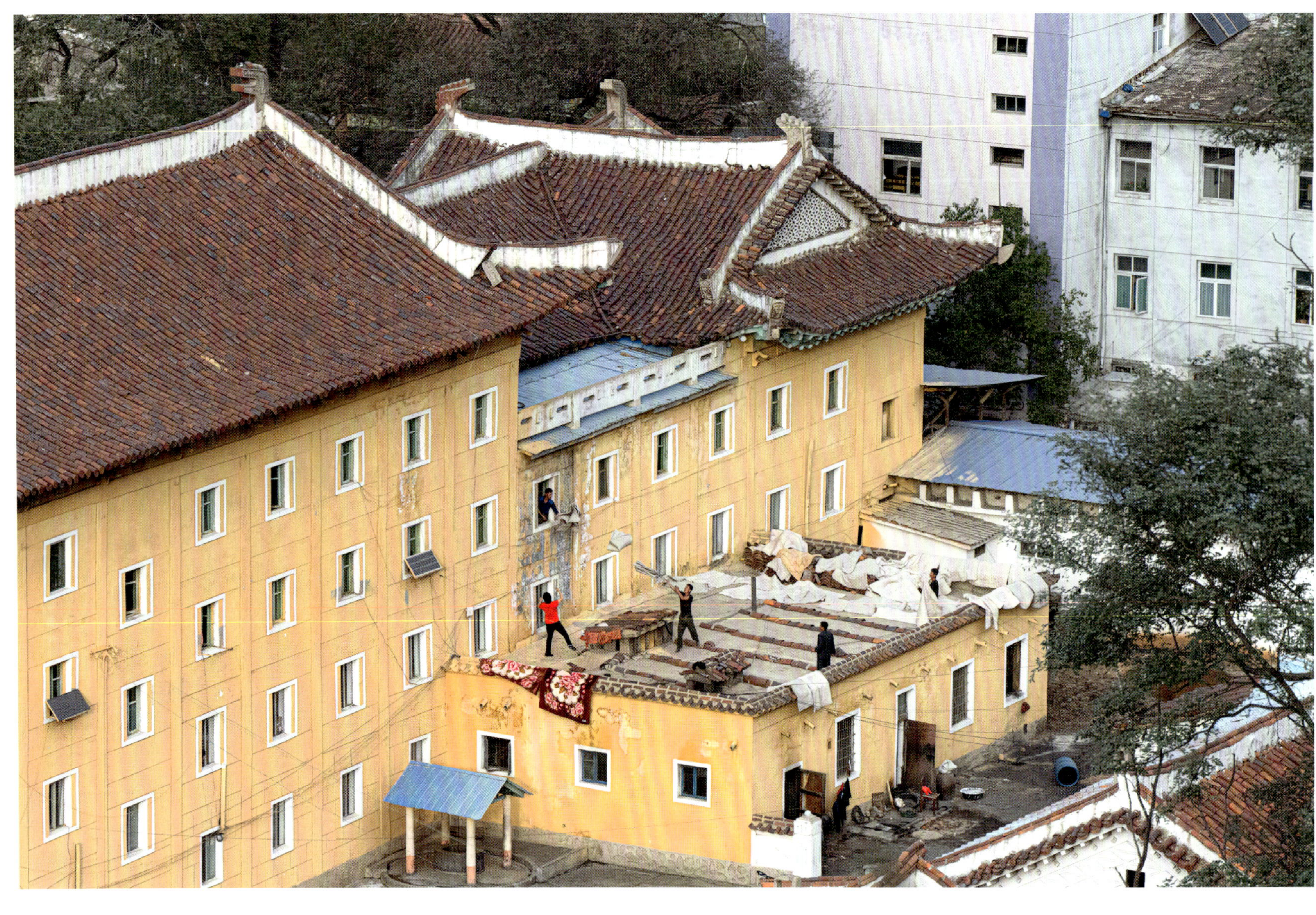

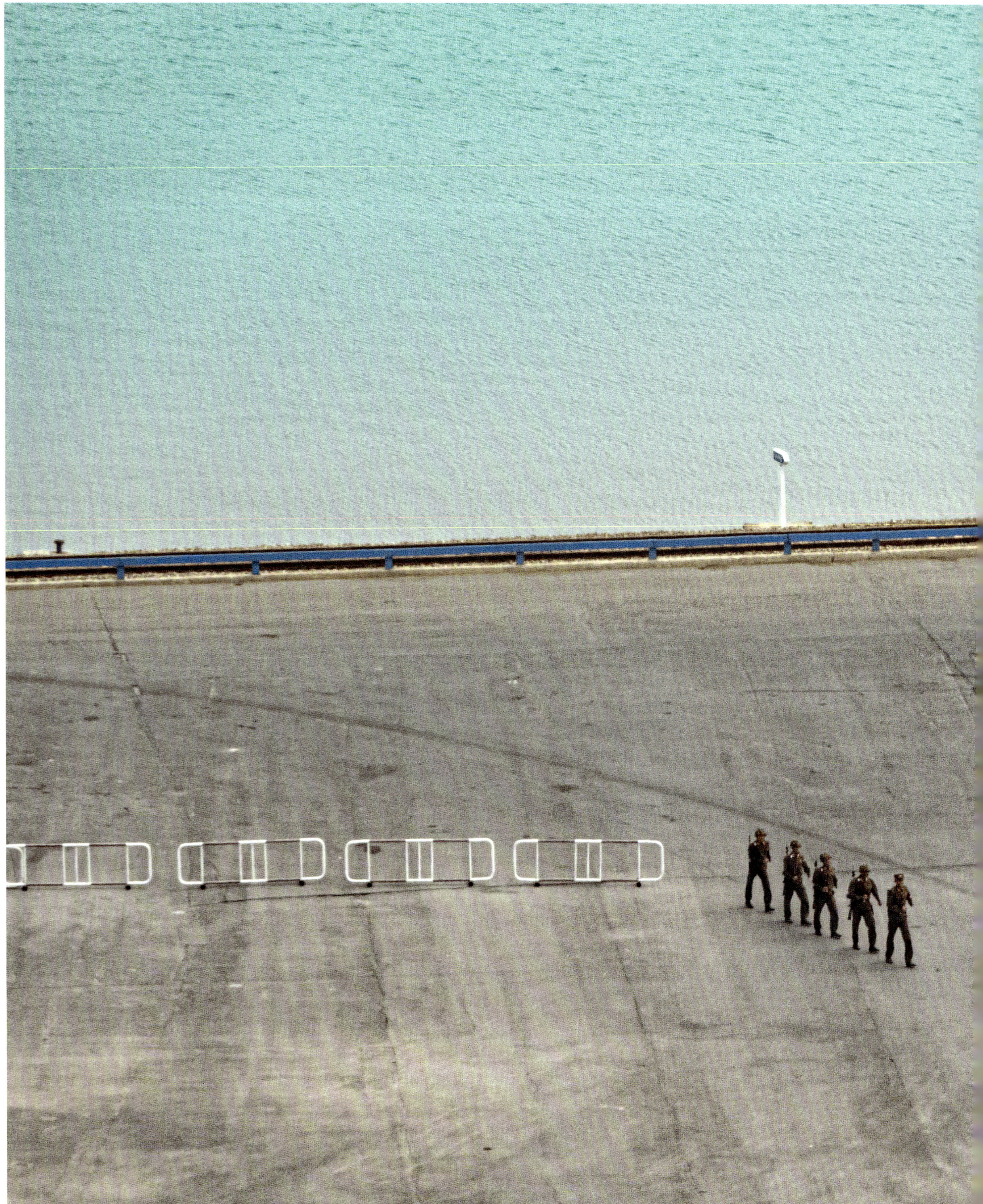

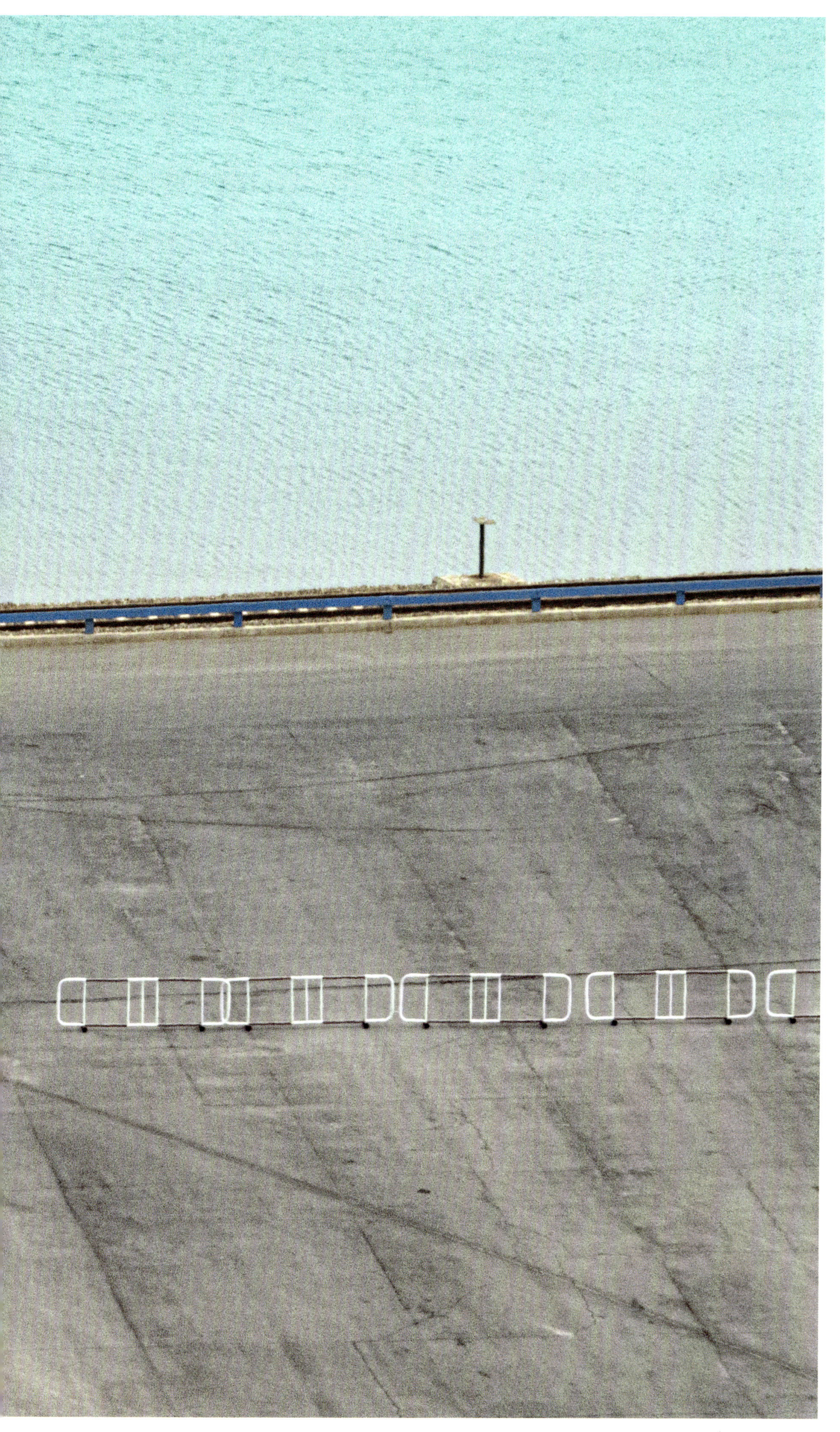

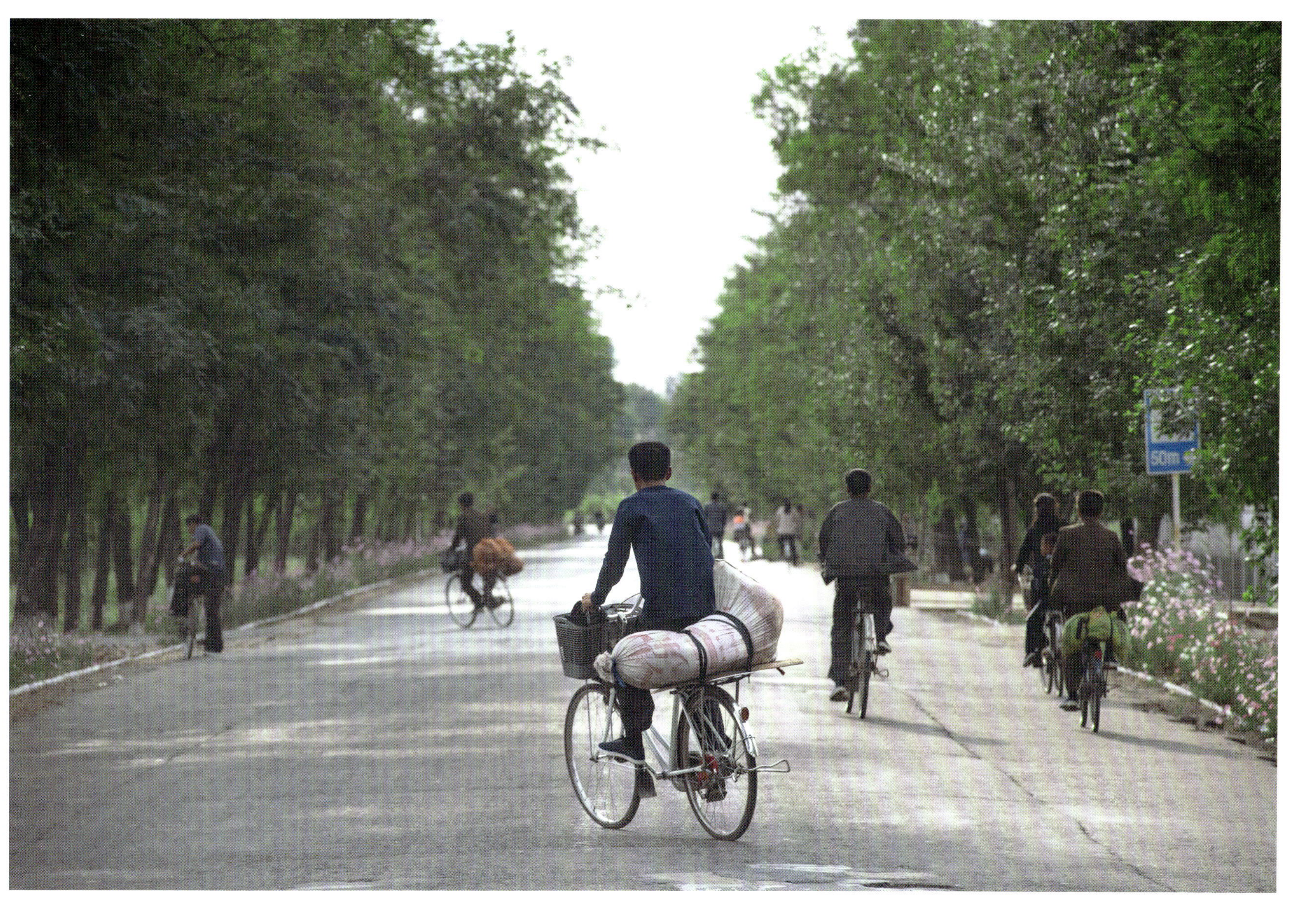

Following our origin in Mount Paektu
Keeping the bloodline alive
By obedience to the sun
Great achievements erupt
Through the name of the leader
Our party will forever shine
For millions of years through the one and only way of Songun
Our Korea will be governed
—from "Let's Give Glory to Our Great Party" (영광을 드리자 위대한 우리 당에)
by The Moranbong Band

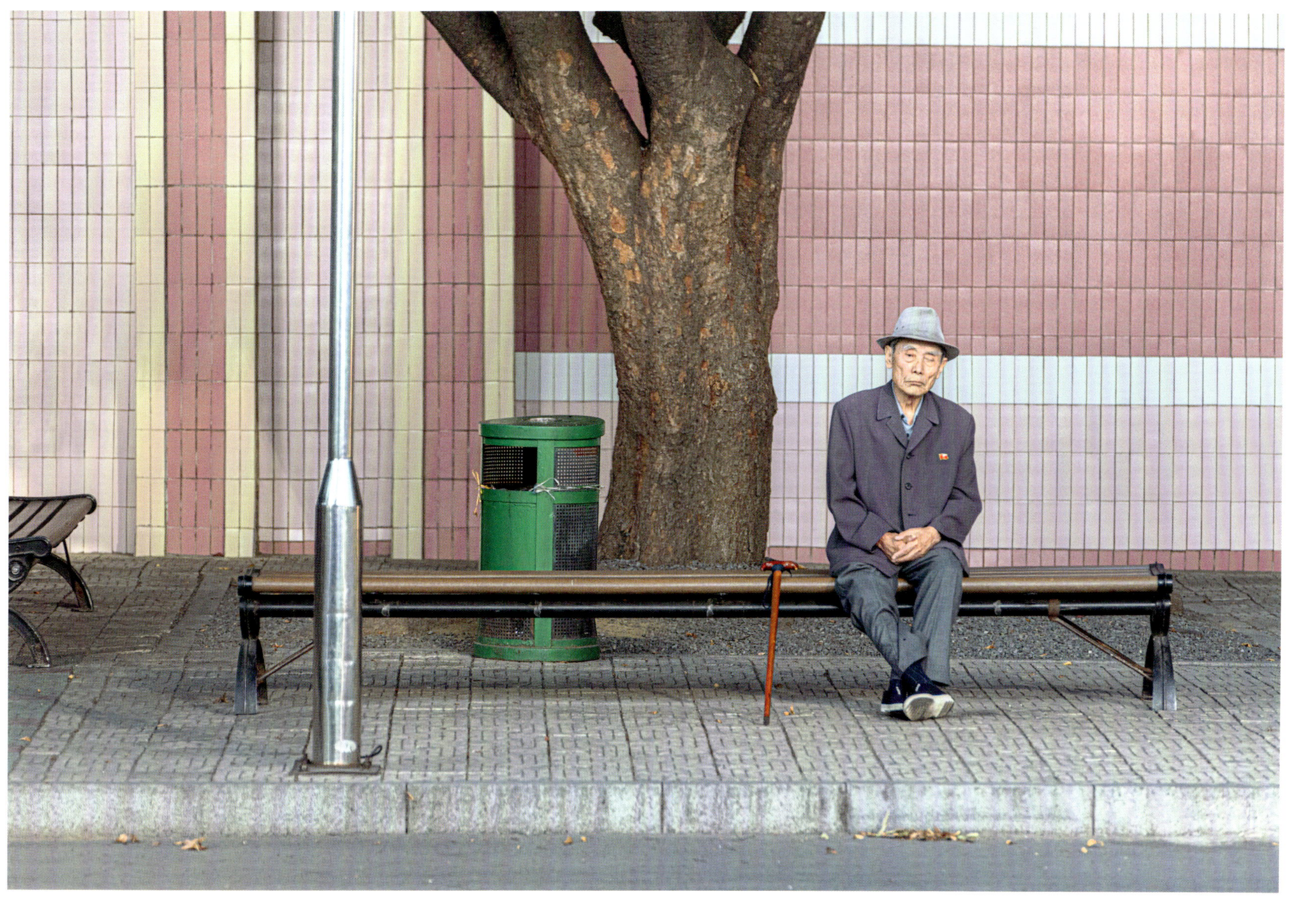

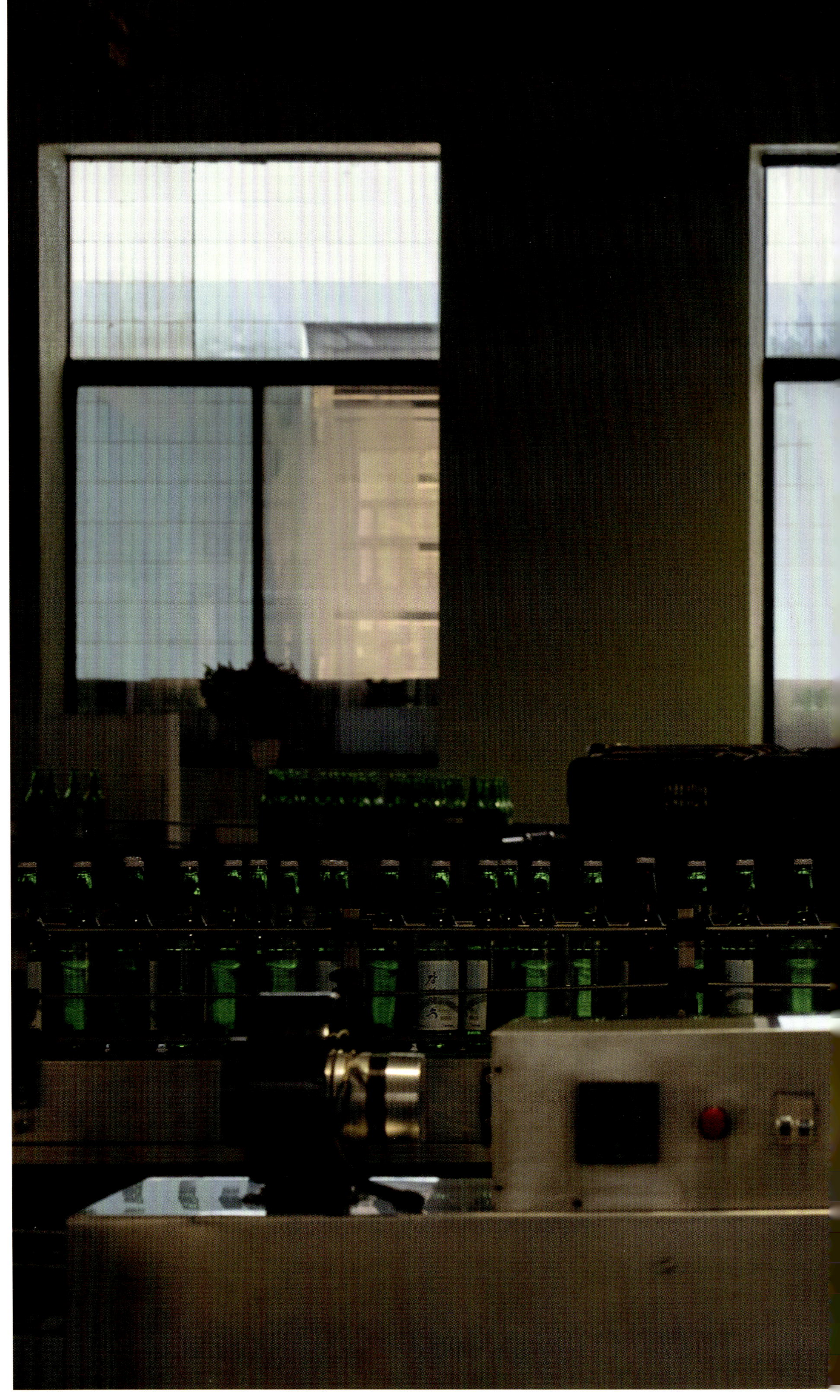

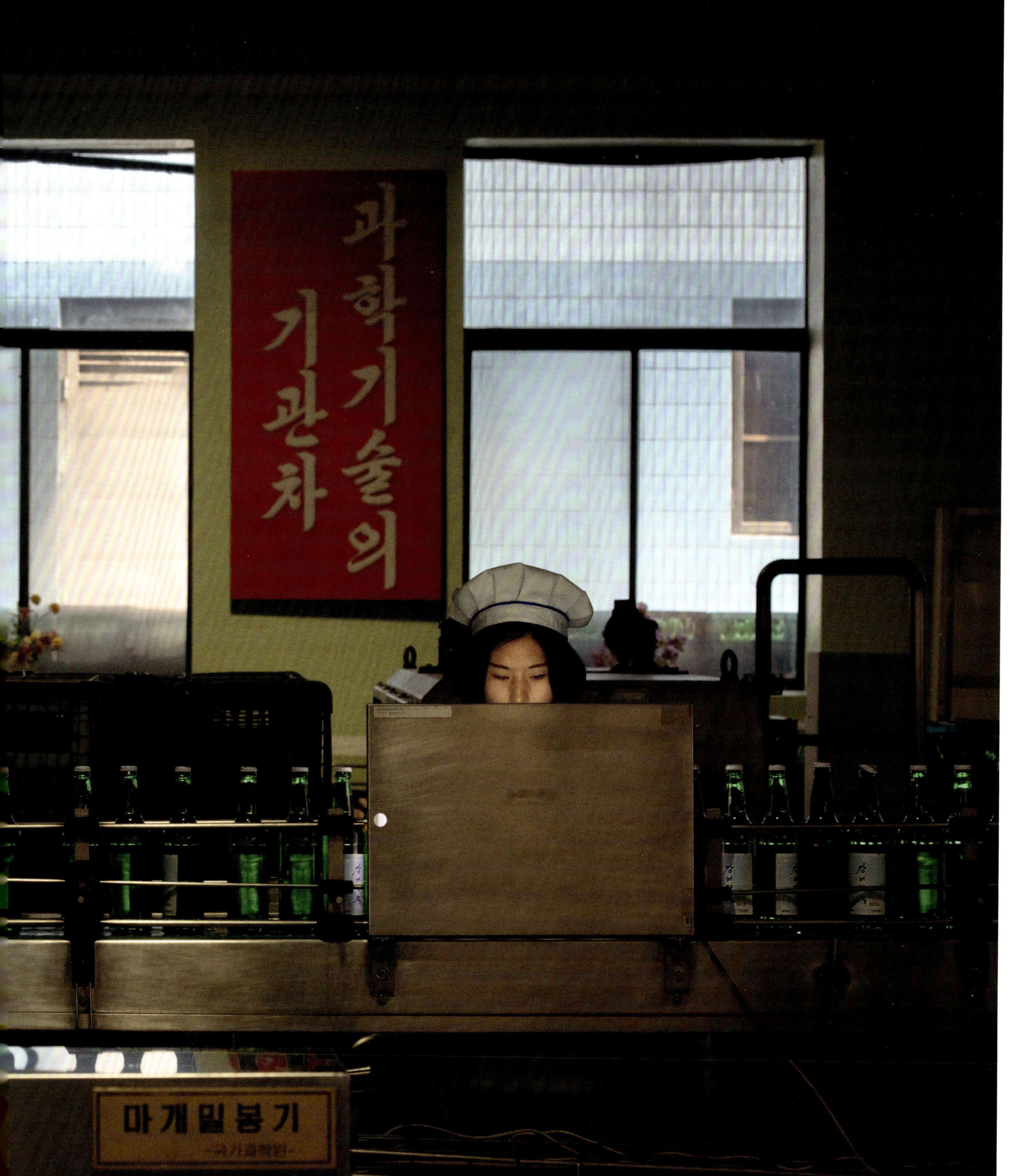

과학기술의
기술의
기관차
마개밀봉기
-국가흑약형-

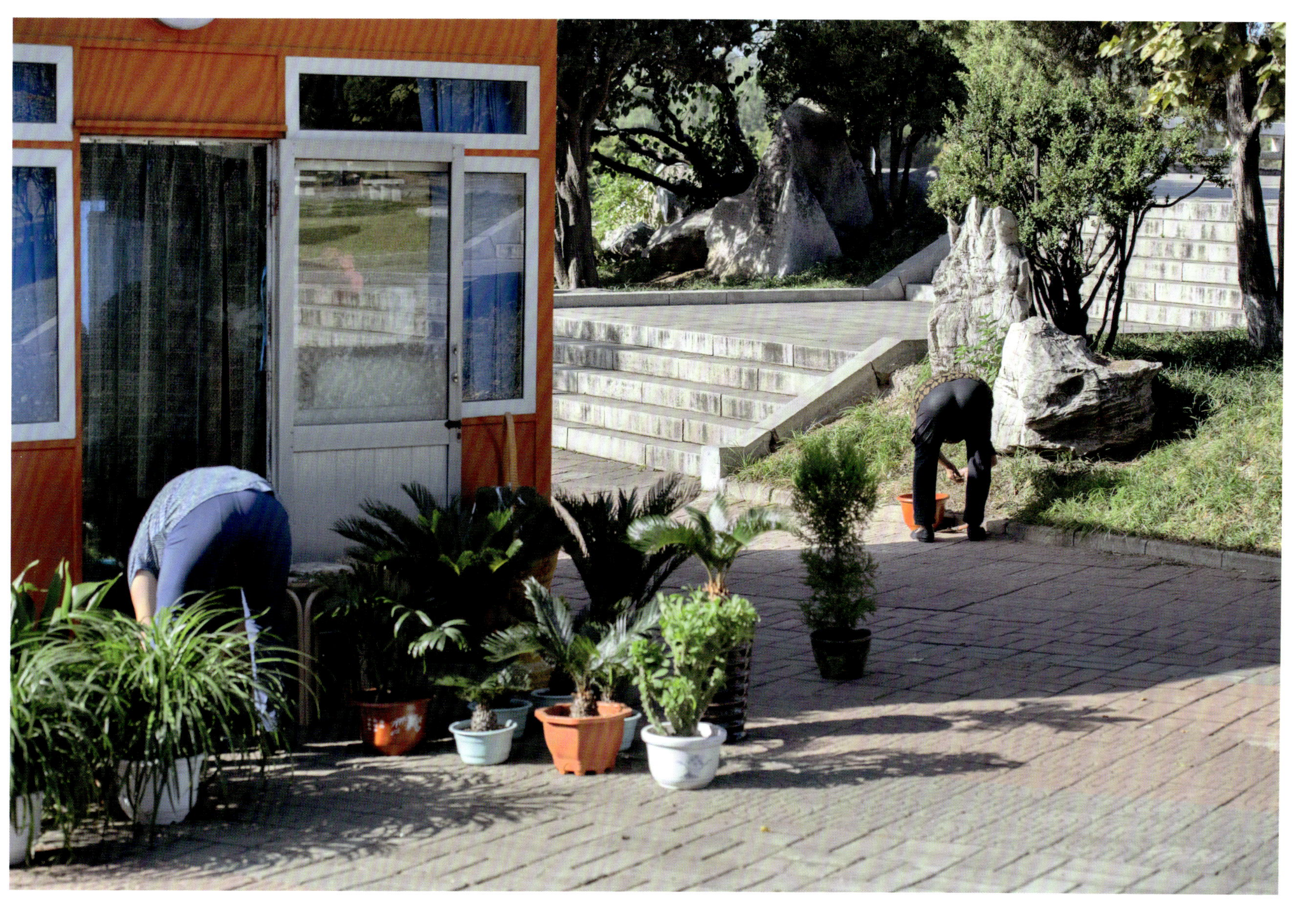

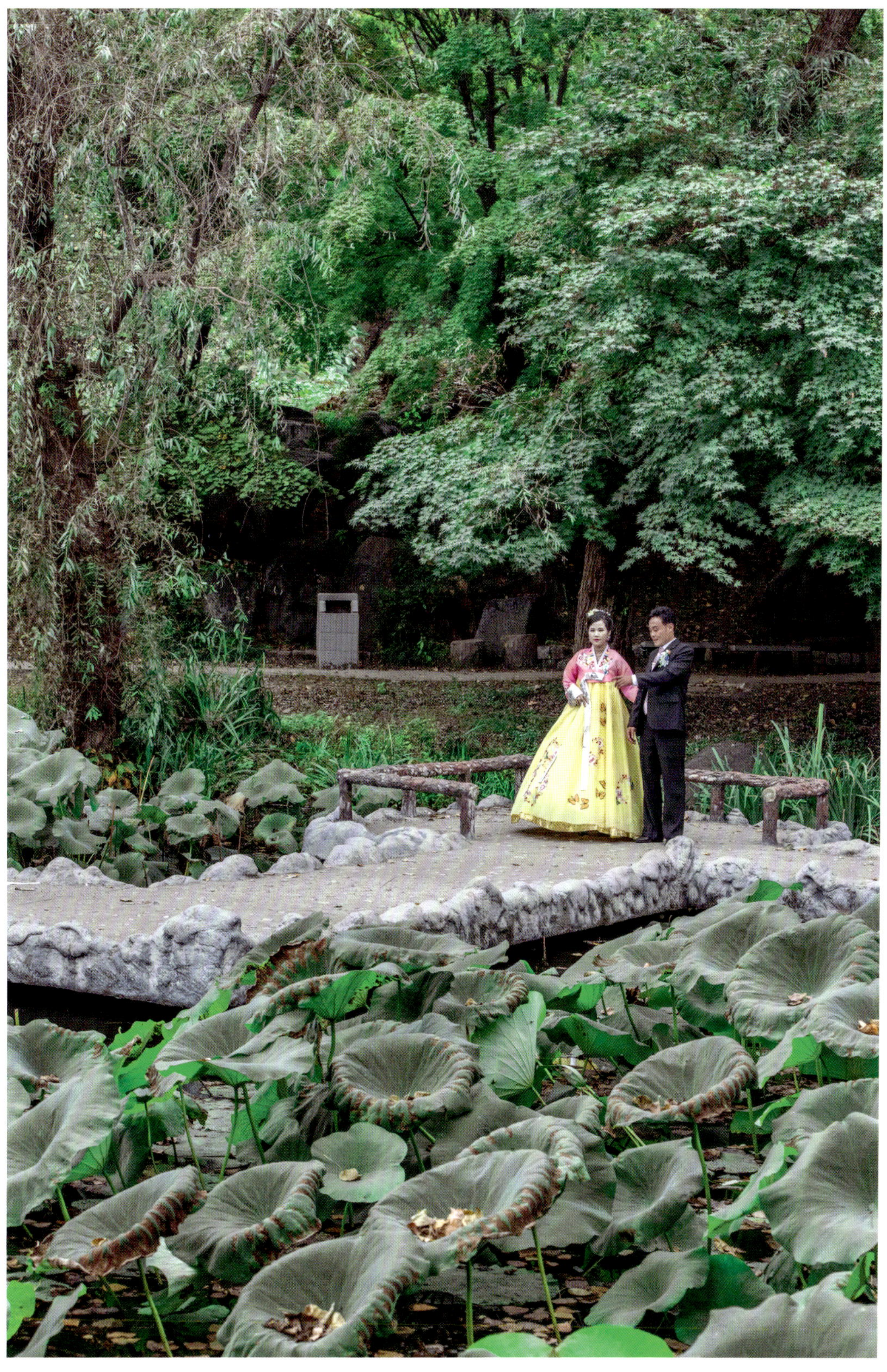

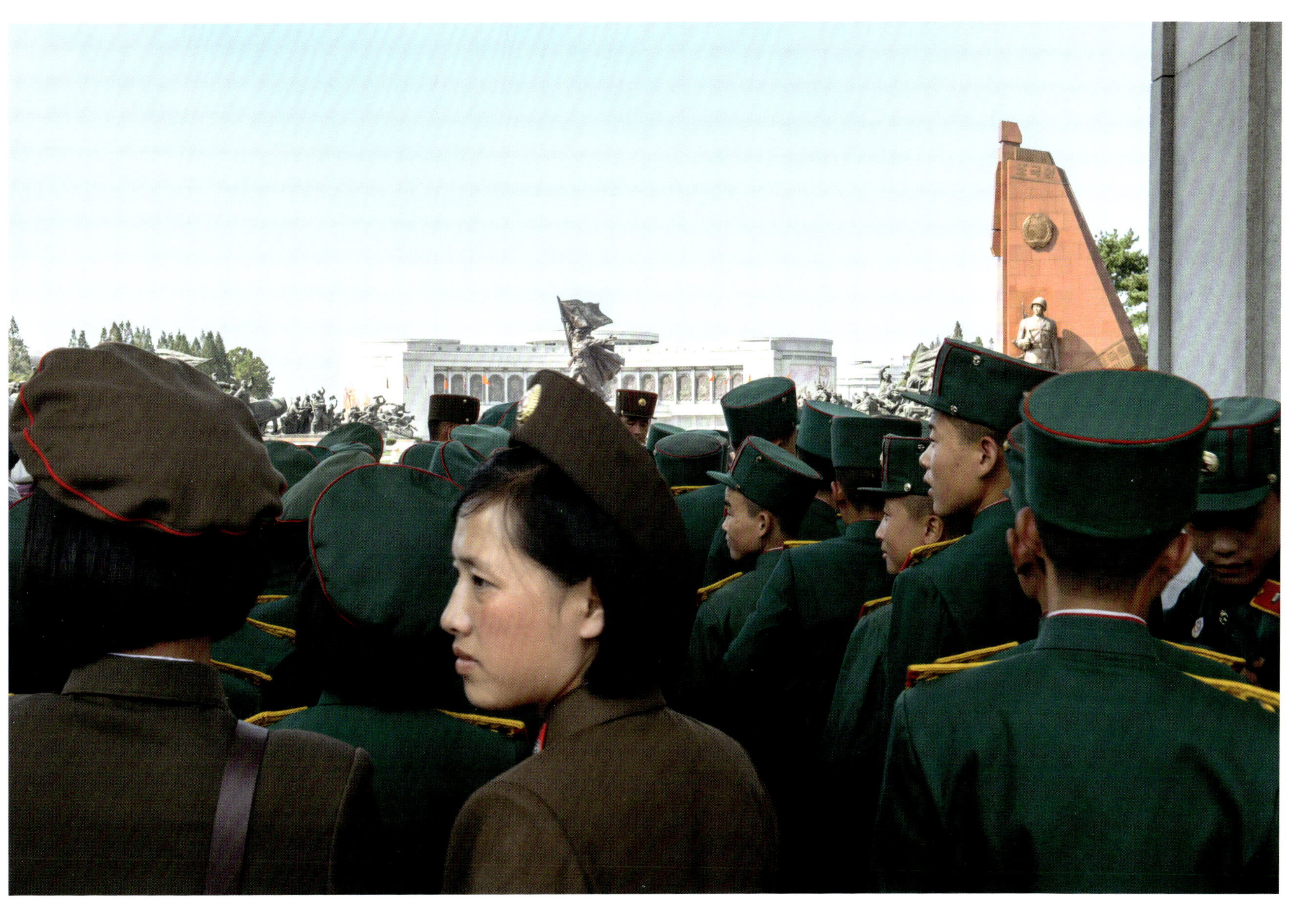

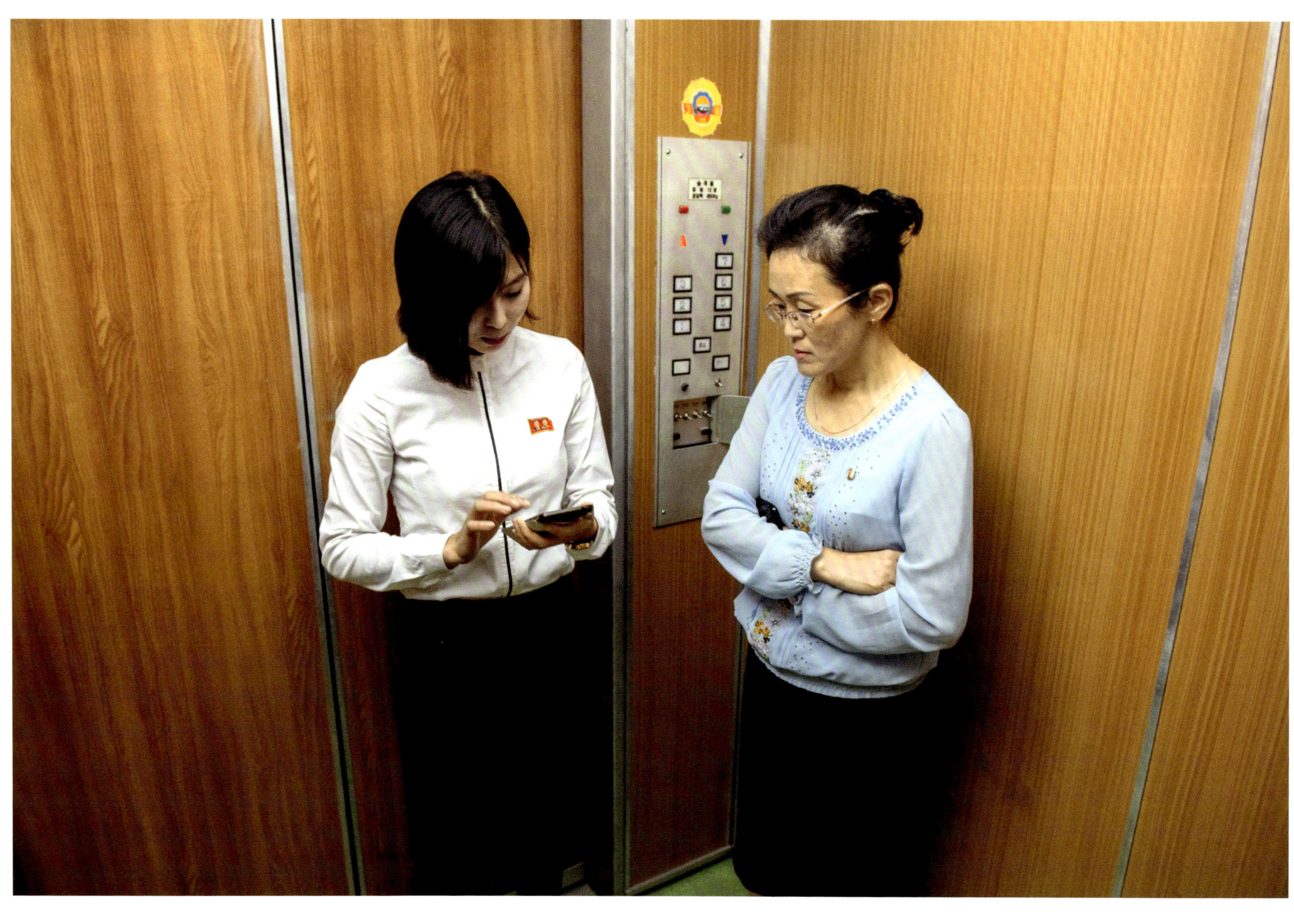

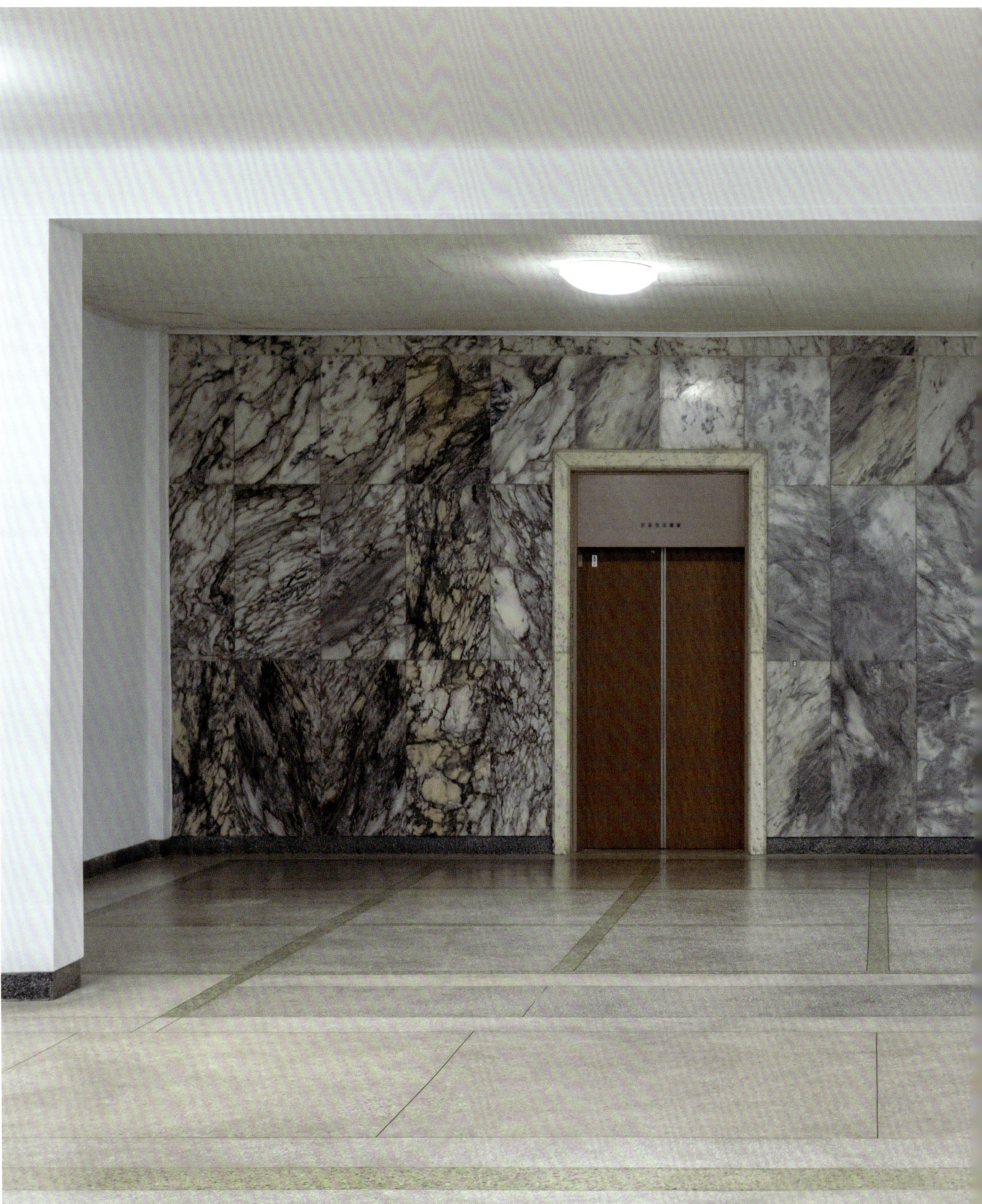

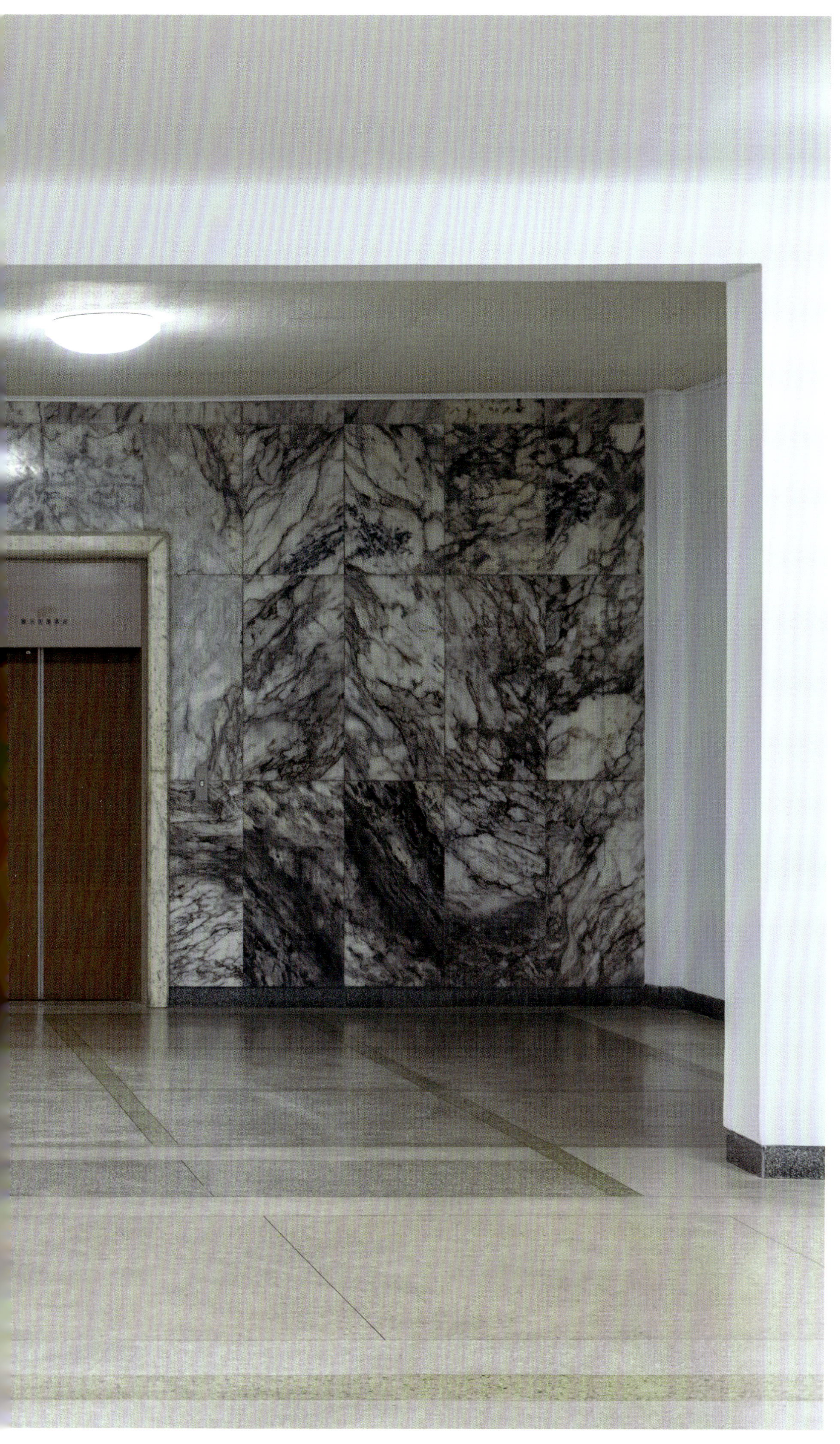

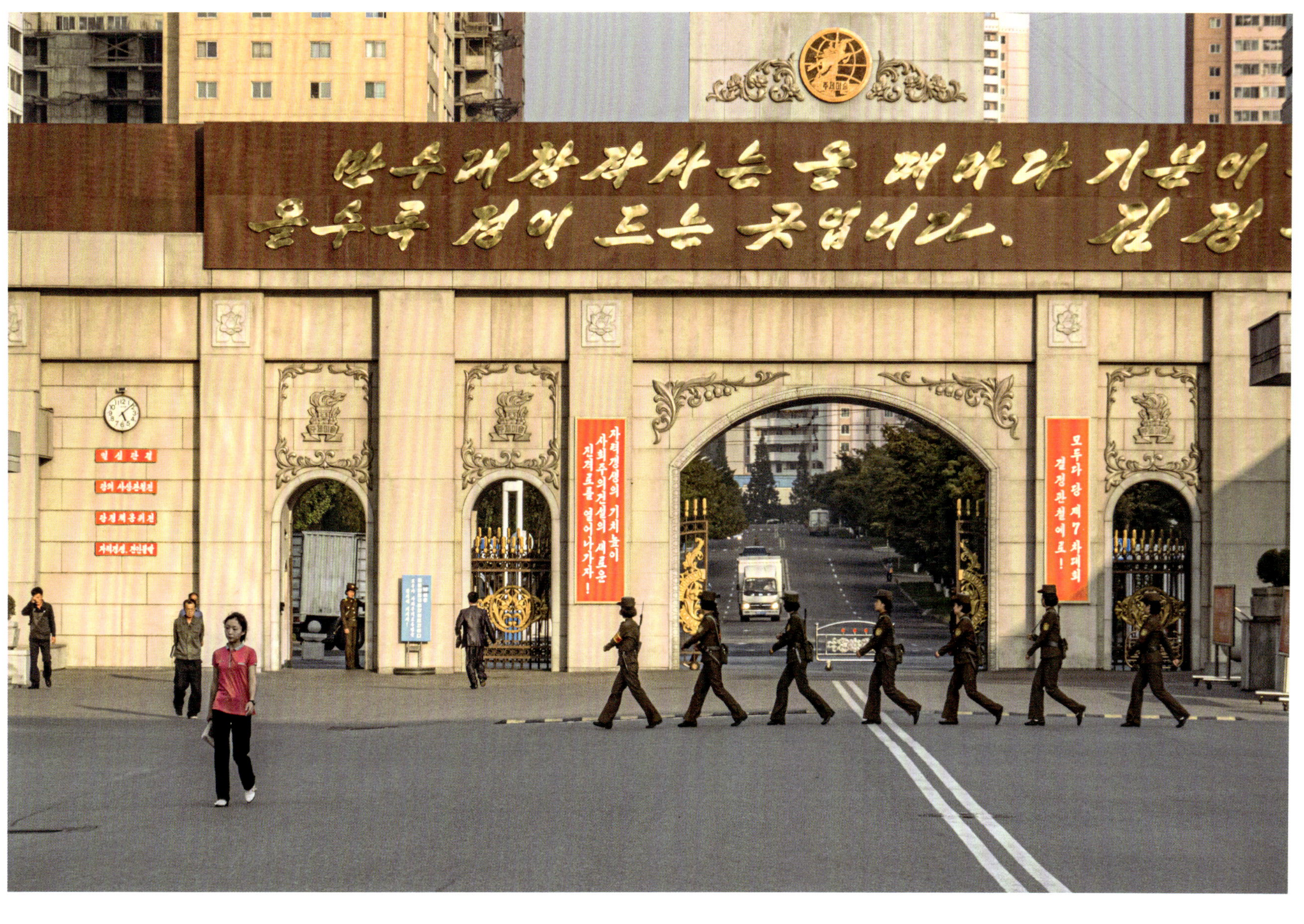

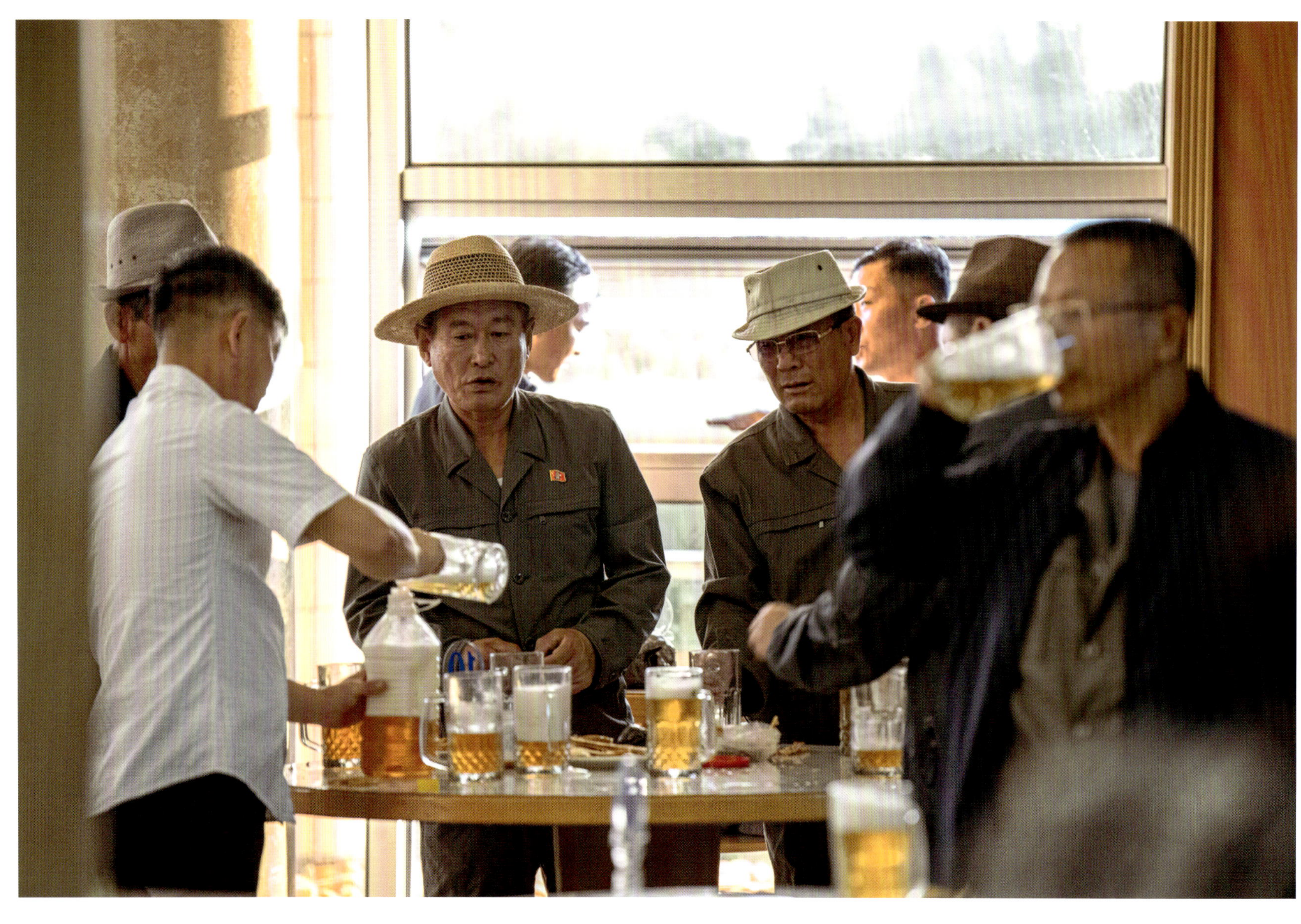

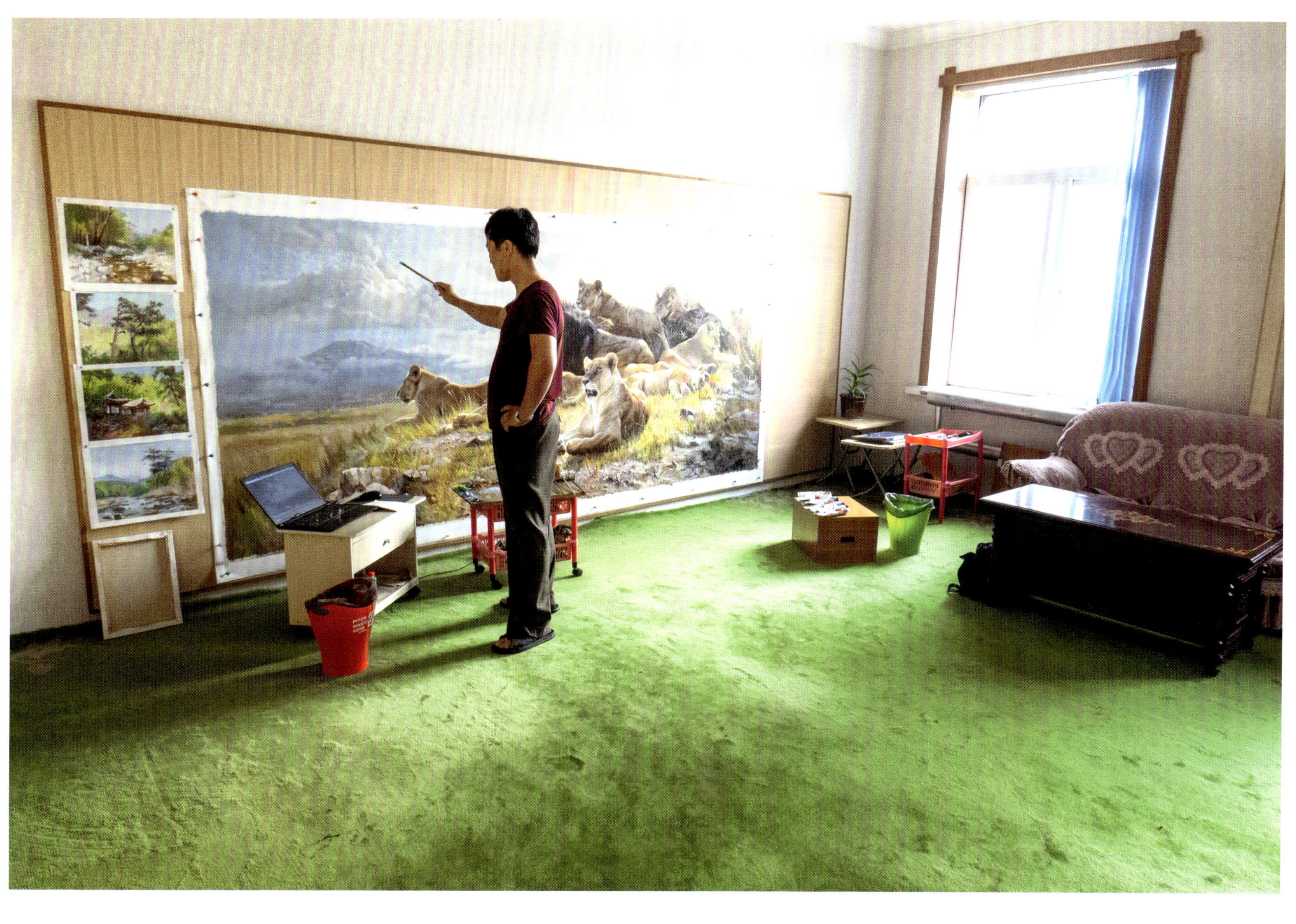

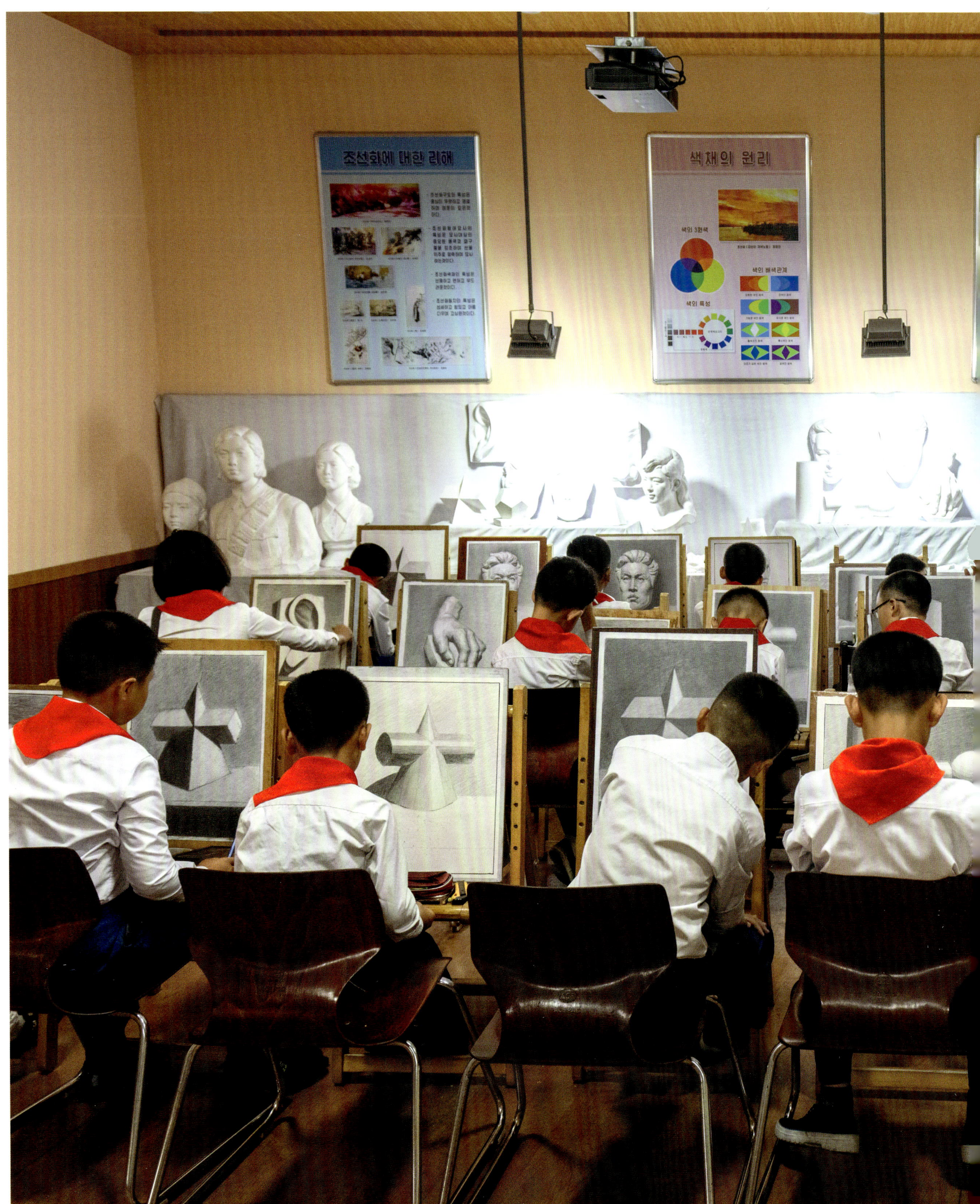

조선화에 대한 리해
색채의 원리
색의 3원색
색의 특성
색의 배색관계

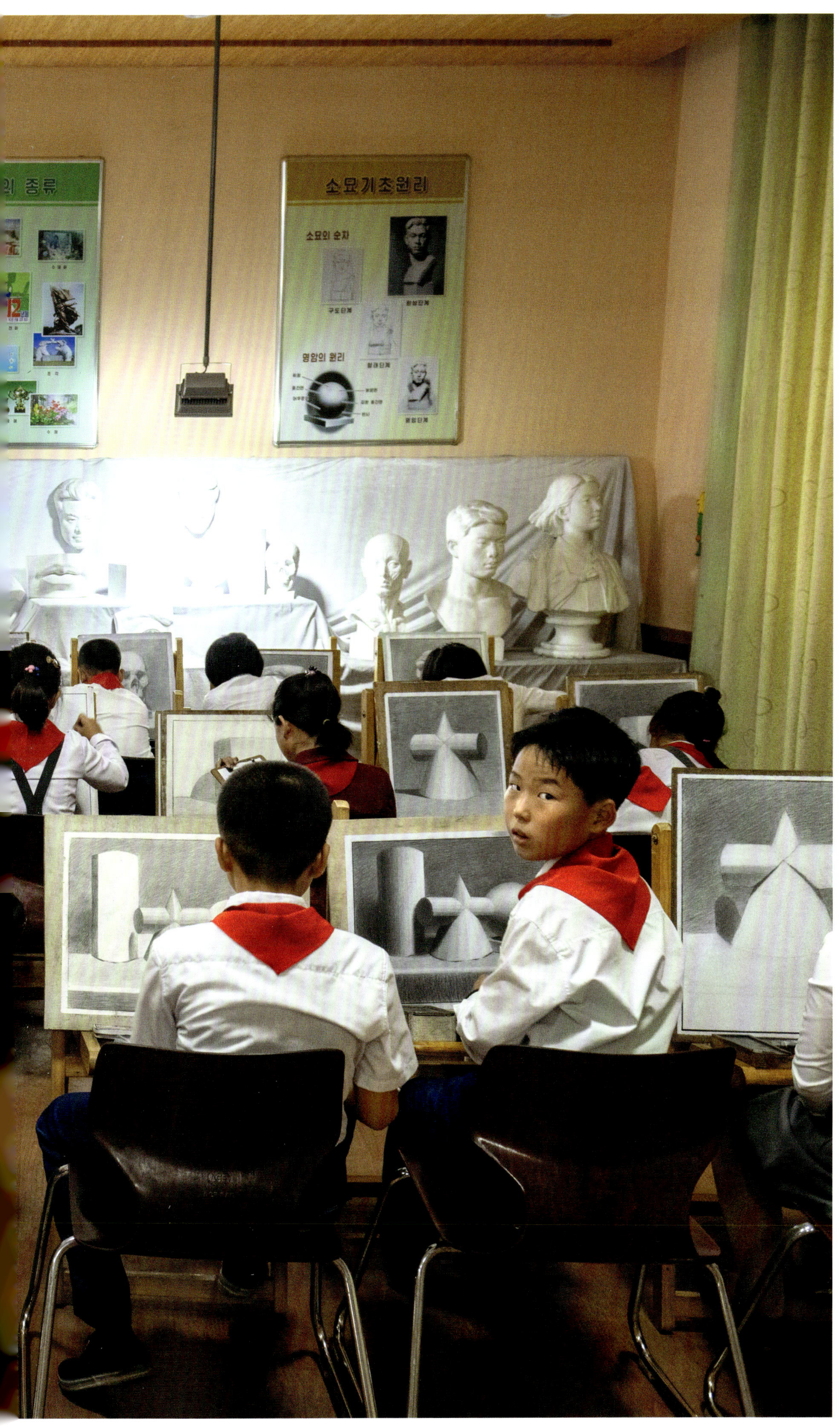
익 종류
소묘기초원리
소묘의 순자
구도단계
완성단계
명암의 원리
명함단계
완성단계

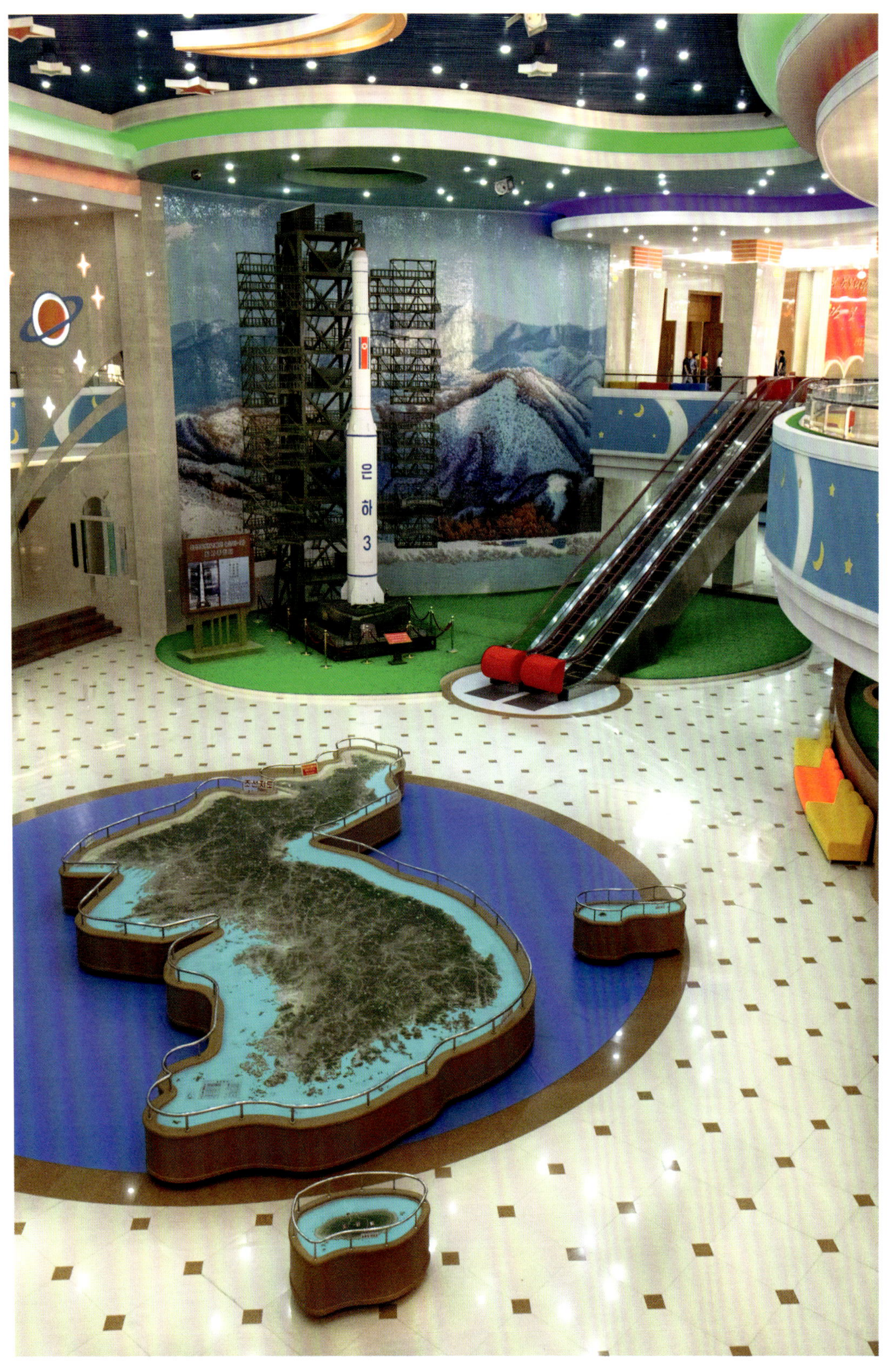

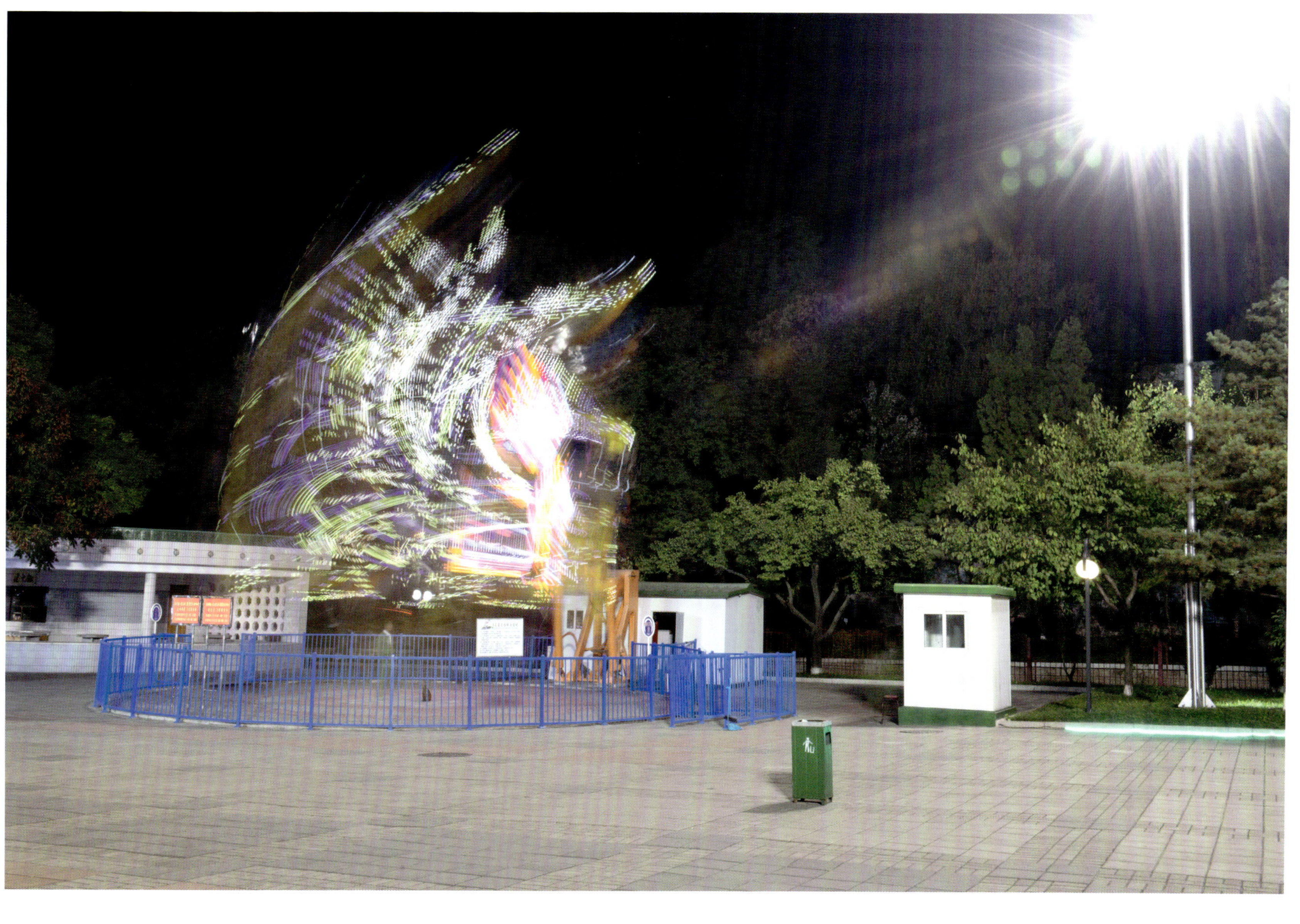

On hilly mountain roads, by air or at sea
Never forgetting the road home in the falling snow
The never-to-be-forgotten days and nights
In the quietly falling snow, the falling snow

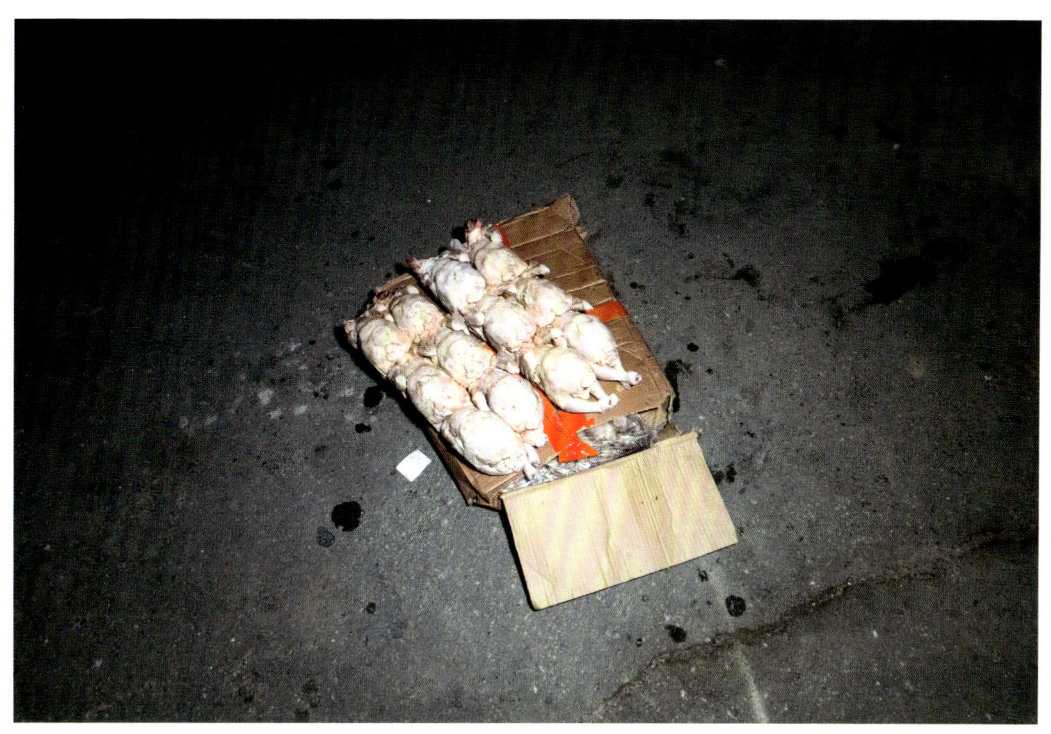

WORK WILL SET YOU FREE: IN THE DPRK

The human mind is a funny thing. As our collective and individual experiences mold and meld themselves into shapely thoughts, our perception of reality shifts too. What might be the truth for one is an outright lie for another. As I write this, and as we find ourselves in the throes of a new world order, my mind wanders to a timely musing, penned 71 years earlier by soothsayer George Orwell: "If you want to keep a secret, you must also hide it from yourself."

Veiled under the garb of nationalism, democratic countries are finding themselves cracking under the tectonic plates of encroaching dictatorships. The largest democracy in the world—India, from where I come—is secretly turning into a totalitarian regime, as the citizens look on with a false sense of pride. The world's alleged top superpower is run by a president who says, "I think if this country gets any kinder or gentler, it's literally going to cease to exist," and the leader of the country that houses Earth's lungs, the Amazon rainforest, is adamant about destroying them.

And still we choose to turn our eyes to North Korea, a fairly tiny country in the Eastern Hemisphere, whispering about the atrocities and human rights violations inflicted upon its people. Popularly known as the "Hermit Kingdom," the land of nearly 26 million citizens remains shrouded in mystery, but clearly has more in common with the world than we'd like to believe.

Here, photographer Ted Lau attempts to uncover the daily lives of the North Korean comrades who may operate with a singular narrative and overwhelming propagandist ideology, but—lest we forget—are still human.

11-13

Contrary to popular belief, tourism is encouraged in North Korea, depending on the passport one holds (American citizens are not permitted to visit the country, as of 2020). For someone who was raised in Hong Kong, aka our photographer, the journey is fairly simple, unless your flight from Beijing is indefinitely delayed due to a dense fog engulfing North Korea's capital, Pyongyang.

As a languid breeze drifts over the seats of Air Koryo, Ted's mind is racing with questions about the mysterious legend of a 70-year-old country run by a communist dynasty.

The "Fatherland" is a carefully crafted vessel that encourages the idea of self-sufficiency, built by Kim Il Sung (president from 1948–1994), his son Kim Jong Il (president from 1994–2011), and grandson and current heir, Kim Jong Un. Brick by brick, public opinion is shaped by the opinion of one, but is portrayed as "decisions made for the collective good of the masses."

While the length and breadth of the country can be viewed as the Kim dynasty's playground, the majority of the population is a willing player in the game. To ensure that visiting foreigners don't disrupt the carefully placed bricks of propaganda, they're assigned two minders/handlers that double as tour guides through the duration of one's trip. The minders even live in the same hotel as their visitors. In Ted's case, Ri and Park were his faithful companions. After all, "the tourists are our guests, and we, the comrades, must ensure a smooth and insightful visit."

14

Translation on building facade:
Thank you, Dear Supreme Leader Kim Jong Un.

17

A painted portrait of Kim Il Sung stands in the foreground of Mount Paektu, at the Grand People's Study House, Pyongyang. According to mythology, the mountain is the spiritual origin of the Korean kingdom, and the alleged birthplace of Kim Il Sung. However, Soviet records show that his actual birthplace was in the Russian Far East village of Vyatskoye.

Every year, approximately one hundred thousand North Koreans visit the holy volcano, donning khaki outfits that resemble guerrilla fighter uniforms, and waving red flags. The pilgrims retrace the steps of Korean revolutionary heroes and fighters while chanting nationalistic songs like "We Will Go to Mount Paektu." For the ones who might not be able to make the journey on foot, there's always the funicular, but that's subject to the electricity gods complying.

20

In this dystopian utopia, there isn't a trace of consumerist and capitalist culture, only the dissemination of ideas. This is evident on the bus stops and billboards that are painted with either important monuments, propagandist slogans ("Let us further glorify socialism of our style on the strength of single-minded unity!"), uplifting scenes of soldiers, or inspirational quotes for the betterment of the working society ("Forging ahead in the twenty-first century").

Seen here is a painted scene of the International Friendship Exhibition, a large museum complex located at Myohyangsan, North Pyongan Province, North Korea. Within its walls lies a collection of halls packed with gifts presented to former leaders Kim Il Sung and Kim Jong Il from various foreign dignitaries. Highlights include Russian bearskins and cars from the 1950s, armored cars from Stalin and Mao, a gold cigarette case from Yugoslavia's Tito, a football signed by Pele, a bronze tank from the USSR headquarters in East Germany, a silver sword encrusted with precious gems from Palestinian leader Yasser Arafat, and an antique gramophone from China's first premier, Zhou Enlai.

Ted and his companion, Yu-Ting Cheng, amusingly recount how the museum guide spoke of rooms packed with gifts from the West. However, they weren't taken through that section, owing to the lack of time.

22-23

A sense of togetherness and herd behavior seeps into the country's transportation system. While the majority of North Korea still heavily relies on bicycles and walking, Pyongyang is buzzing with public transport in the form of electric train carriages, trams, and buses. It is here that the country's most loyal comrades thrive, collectively journeying toward their six-day working weeks. While tourists are ferried around in private vehicles, far removed from the lives of the locals, curious sights dance through glass windows. Vintage Hungarian buses from the 1950s drift along roads from the future, and are painted with different stars. Each star stands for five thousand accident-free miles, denoting behavior worthy of an award. The gaze of the smiling leaders is omnipresent, unavoidable, and keeps the citizens in check. Here, Orwell's words resound once again: "Big Brother is watching you."

25

The theatrical city of Pyongyang was completely rebuilt post-1953, after being flattened by US bombing during the Korean War. For a country whose air is still dense with characteristics from the Soviet Union, Pyongyang reeks of futuristic facades and Jetson-like skyscrapers. While the east side of the city is packed with colorful Soviet-style concrete apartment blocks, the west side is filled with grand buildings, stadiums, and newer developments. The two are separated by the mighty Taedong River.

Prior to the Korean War, architecture in the city was rather gray. But under orders of Kim Jong Il, the country was splashed with minty greens, lemon yellows, sky blues, and neon and baby pinks.

One wonders if the candy-land packaging is also a means of propaganda, spreading an atmosphere of utopia amongst the population.

Ted captured this scene from atop the Grand People's Study House, which overlooks Kim Il Sung Square. The photographer observed a large number of chalk markings scattered across the square, which are made for the impressive military parades synonymous with the country. Within the Study House, a special parapet exists for the Leaders, from where they watch these largely synchronized and colorful performances.

27-28

It's fairly easy to be impressed by the larger-than-life sights in Pyongyang, a place dotted with massive bronze statues of leaders and citizens alike. The leaders are consistently depicted as benevolent fathers rather than austere rulers. Here, a worker, a farmer, and an intellectual clutch a hammer, sickle, and calligraphy brush, to represent the Korean Workers' Party. Much like everything in this highly sanitized land, the mammoth statues are permanently shining. And still, no tourist or citizen has ever seen them being maintained.

Flanking the statue that represents the holy trifecta of a North Korean citizen stands the 170-meters-high Juche Tower. It was opened in 1982 to commemorate the 70th birthday of Kim Il Sung, who is responsible for an ideology that runs deep within the veins of every North Korean comrade.

> "Establishing *Juche* means, in a nutshell, being the master of revolution and reconstruction in one's own country. This means holding fast to an independent position, rejecting dependence on others, using one's own brains, believing in one's own strength, displaying the revolutionary spirit of self-reliance, and thus solving one's own problems for oneself on one's own responsibility under all circumstances."
> —Kim Il Sung

The idea of self-reliance has proven successful. The citizens truly believe that their country is the most powerful, their leader is much revered, and that under the leadership of Kim Jong Un, the North Korean government has developed a wonder drug that can cure both AIDS and Ebola.

There is a continuous sense of surveillance, and ideology precedes reality. Ted was privy to this first-hand: As he casually commented on the noticeable fumes emanating from a power plant, his minders were quick to retort, "What fumes?"

32-39

There isn't any aspect of the country that isn't meticulously organized. That's probably why the elaborate Pyongyang subway stations, inspired by those in Soviet Moscow, are dug deep enough to survive a nuclear attack. Since nuclear war with the United States is a fairly common topic discussed at a North Korean dinner table, the capital attempts to stay equipped amidst the looming threats. Long corridors with huge metal gates at either end safeguard the fate of a small percentage of the country, who use the two metro lines to travel within the city.

Ted was especially captivated by the cotton-candy pink that engulfs the recently renovated Kaeson metro station. The line that leads toward the Arch of Triumph could be a frame straight out of a Wes Anderson film, if not for the revolutionary music and patriotic songs constantly playing along its escalators.

Apart from the usual photographs and sculptures of the Dear Leaders, the subways are lined with elaborate chandeliers, mosaics, propagandist scenes depicted in bronze, and ornate columns. It isn't uncommon to see North Koreans huddled together reading the *Rodong Sinmun*, the official paper of the Korean Workers' Party that's always on display in the metro.

Though the *Sinmun* has the largest circulation in the country, you'll find a variety of other newspapers such as the *Pyongyang News, Sports News,* and *Children's Union News.* On October 2, 2019, during our photographer's visit, North Korea fired a ballistic missile from a submarine. Visuals from the launch were plastered all over the subway news.

Ted also speaks about the commonality of tiny red badges worn by North Korean citizens, seen glinting under the subway lights. Throughout the country, but especially in Pyongyang, comrades roam with badges depicting their leaders' faces from different eras. The pins cannot be bought by tourists and are usually given as gifts by officials or family members after a particular life goal is achieved. The minders explain that the badges are worn on the left side of the chest, so that the leaders are always close to one's heart.

Apart from the sight of the red badges, which is more noticeable because of the concentrated population in the metro, Ted's eyes fall upon English alphabets, quotes, and words scribbled onto the interiors of the train with either keys or coins. Ri explains that these are remnants from the Dora trains produced in West Berlin between 1957 and 1965, and withdrawn from German service in 1999. North Korea now possesses these carriages, along with a rise in more domestically produced metro cars.

40-55

The atmosphere is electric at the Rungrado May Day Stadium in Pyongyang, which holds the record for the largest stadium in the world (seating capacity: 150,000). It's finally time for the hugely popular Arirang Mass Games, which inspired Ted to make a trip to the Hermit Kingdom. Known to be the largest performance of theater, artistry, gymnastics, and propaganda stories in the world, the games are well-attended by locals and throngs of Chinese tourists. The photographer describes the atmosphere as energetic, brimming with nationalistic pride, and uneasy, because even here, they are being watched.

Along with the Juche ideology that governs the daily lives of the people, North Koreans also reiterate that nothing is impossible if it's done together. The painstakingly curated games are named after a North Korean folk song that tells the story of star-crossed lovers who are cruelly separated by fate. The tale alludes, in a not-so-subtle way, to the division of the two Koreas, and the North's desperate yearning for reunification.

First introduced in 2002, the annual spectacle took a five-year hiatus from 2013 until 2018. This, too, was shrouded in mystery, as the government provided no official explanation for the sudden break. However, the ninety-minute synchronized gymnastics made a comeback in 2018, and celebrated the 70th anniversary of the country's foundation. The games were kick-started with a patriotic song titled "Shining Fatherland," performed by Kim Jong Un's hand-picked girl group, Moranbong Band.

Over the years, one hundred thousand young, strong, and agile North Koreans have been carefully selected from districts across Pyongyang to spend eight months in intensive practice sessions. Even though the performances might change, the themes are largely based on the struggles against the Japanese, the division of Korea, the benevolence of the leaders, and the advantages of socialism. Here, even the clapping is surprisingly in unison, displaying the same pace of colliding hands and wide-eyed expressions.

Ted was particularly impressed by the segments depicting North Korea's nuclear energy program, and of course, the highlight of the show, which centers around rows of students taking on the avatar of a human canvas. The participants in the stands act as human pixels who flip colorful cards to reveal life-sized mosaics and slogans. With the help of a two-hundred-page flipbook, the students flit between static and dynamic images that transition before the spectator has the time to blink.

Last year's games caused the photographer a fair bit of anxiety, since they almost didn't happen. Kim Jong Un indefinitely suspended the festival after its opening in June 2018, as the performances didn't meet his standards. He criticized them for having "the wrong spirit of creation," and propagating an "irresponsible work attitude." However, before Ted's scheduled trip in October, the spectacle was thankfully up and running.

57-59

As you step across the border of Pyongyang, and into the expanse of the countryside, the well-masked petroleum sanctions are suddenly apparent. The smooth roads of the capital have transformed into bumpy and rough asphalt pathways strewn with cracks. En route to the International Friendship Exhibition, across the special four-lane highway, Ted watches his driver Kim dodge the potholes with ease. In the back of the car, the photographer clenches his back to decrease the impact of the bumps, and tries to produce a steady photograph.

North Korea has been under international sanctions since the late 1950s to punish the regime for cyberattacks, money laundering, and human rights violations. In 2006, the United Nations posed additional sanctions of military and technological materials, petroleum, natural gas imports, as well as financial sanctions, owing to the country's erratic nuclear and ballistic missile programs.

Even though eighty-five percent of the country's population lives outside of the capital, the majority of available funds are directed toward Pyongyang. Appearance is everything. And yet the citizens still proudly declare North Korea a paradise on Earth, and casually deem it the strongest country in the world. They also trust that imports have to be avoided because of the strategies of the country's enemies, who can use the resources to attack the fabric of their proud nation.

> *The morning light is so fine,*
> *In our land of morning calm!*
> *Our country is so beautiful,*
> *Where else in the world can you find such a beautiful land?*
>   —Song taught in school; translation from Korean to English

On their journey to the seaport town of Nampo, Ted notices that there is barely any unharvested land in the countryside. Farmers huddle in groups of ten, manually harvesting the hectares of rice, wheat, barley, millet, and buckwheat fields. The farmers are the hardest workers, maintaining a routine of nine working days, with one day off. Depending on the amount they reap per month, they are given food stamps by the government. At times when their harvest fails, the family starves, with no alternatives available.

However, the farmers often believe that in a socialist society, a person who doesn't work shouldn't be able to eat. To quote a farmer interviewed in Sung-Hyung Cho's documentary *My Brothers and Sisters in the North* (2016), "If the State is rich and strong, then the individuals have a good life too. The stronger the State is, the less likely it is that the imperialists will attack us."

The rural population is most grateful to the leaders who have visited them in the past. "In which other country does a leader visit a field?" continues the overwhelmed farmer. However, they are oblivious to the fact that in the 1990s, at the height of a famine that claimed two million lives, Kim Jong Il was the single biggest customer for Hennessy cognac in the world. Documentary footage from the famine, or "The Arduous March," shows children plastered with rouge on their faces, to suggest that they are indeed healthy and not suffering from malnutrition. At the same time, cotton clothing was branded "unfashionable," even though the real reason it was declared so was the absolute lack of the fabric.

60

Through my research, conversations with Ted and Cheng, and interviews with North Korean experts, I notice that there's an underlying pattern that exists within their experiences. Since tours are so highly structured, the sites to visit, opinions, behavior, and illuminations are almost identical. Here, tourism is also a form of propaganda, which the North Koreans believe is a means of education.

To further propagate this thought, visitors are taken to the West Sea Barrage, an expansive dam located nine miles west of Nampo. Flanked by a pair of statues of the workers who built it, this symbol of North Korean communism separates the Yellow Sea from the Taedong River. Built between 1981 and 1986 by thirty thousand soldiers and thousands of civilians, the dam cost more than $1.8 billion. For a country that was battling a famine, and struggling with allocating funds for its own citizens, it seemed like a bold feat. But for a land whose national emblem is a giant hydroelectric station, it's not a surprising one.

On visiting, Ted was ferried atop a lighthouse, where he was shown a black-and-white film in Korean about the building of this dam, and Kim Jong Il's invaluable expertise during its construction. Even though it's definitely curious how a leader could advise specialists in matters of science and engineering, the narrative stresses the fact that it was he who guided the workers through their difficulties. The monuments scattered across the country hold a sense of Korean nationalism and stand as reflections of the comrades' diligence and hard work.

The West Sea Barrage is commonly seen as a backdrop on North Korean television news broadcasts, and the dam's official poem is synonymous with North Korean attitudes of self-reliance and pride:

> *O shine for all centuries to come,*
> *Great monument of the '80s built*
> *By our design, our technique, our strength;*

Daily patrolling and multiple tours are common sights at this quiet and languid place. Ted and Cheng were promised a picnic, which to their surprise took place in an indoor restaurant at the Hangu Harbour Hotel. They binged on the North Korean version of a traditional fast-food meal, which consisted of crunchy fried chicken, fries, and King Cola (the country's take on Coca-Cola).

63
Nampo.

64
An hour and a half away from Pyongyang lies Sariwon, the capital of North Hwanghae province. Ted trekked up the tallest hill in the district and was greeted with a view of this bright yellow building, presumably a hotel. The simple act of shuttling drying sheets into a mysterious structure intrigued him and he raised his camera to take a photograph. However, Ri requested he delete the frame, since it wasn't very "nice" and didn't adhere to the image of the country.

According to the rules of the land, photographing workers, construction sites, and soldiers is forbidden.

66-67
Military patrolling at the West Sea Barrage.

69
Outside of Pyongyang, cycles, walking, and a handful of intercity buses are the limited ways of moving around. Ted was discouraged from making this photograph of locals returning home from work.

72-73
The Kangso Mineral Water Factory in Nampo is advertised as home to the DPRK's most famous sparkling water, Yaksu. Since showcasing their industrial prowess is high up on North Korea's agenda, the factory is a stop on most tourist itineraries. Apart from showing off their Italian machinery, the factory also stocks foreign sparkling water to compare the quality.

Legend has it that a local farmer once witnessed a sick crane drinking from a pond and saw it miraculously recover afterward. Since then, Kangso has been considered to have magical water flowing from its depths.

Within the factory, Ted spots motivational slogans plastered across the walls. He also notices that there is a variation in the production of glass bottles, since it's possible to randomly come across an old beer bottle being recycled for mineral water.

Cheng is most amused by the fact that the factory boasts of controlling their carbonated bubbles, depending on the countries they are catering to. They proudly talk about reducing bubble content when exporting to South Asian countries, and increasing it when supplying to Europe.

77

Love drifts through Korean air at the Moranbong park located in central Pyongyang. Amidst the lakes, floating streams, and clusters of colorful flowers, newly married couples wearing traditional *hanbok* dresses flock to immortalize their special day in this cavern of green. While some lovers strike more standard poses, it isn't uncommon to see heavily staged scenes involving blowing bubbles, playing with tiny waterfalls, and a groom running toward his bride multiple times with a bright red rose in his hand, for the perfect shot.

Weddings usually take place between late October, when the farming season has ended, and February. However, it's important to keep in mind that no ceremonies can be planned on April 15 or February 16—the birthdays of the former leaders.

Arranged marriages, or *seon*, are more common than love-based marriages here, and weddings have recently become fairly grand and expensive affairs. The "ideal" partners are sifted from Party workers and military services, or are comrades with higher-education backgrounds. Laborers and farmers who can't afford gifts or lavish buffets pay vendors for wedding essentials, take photographs for posterity, and then return the goods after use.

According to tradition, the newlyweds immediately visit the Mansudae Grand Monument, a memorial standing seventy-two-feet high and notable for its bronze statues of Kim Il Sung and Kim Jong Il. Flowers are offered at the feet of the omnipresent leaders, which North Koreans believe makes the marriage eternally blessed.

79

"Every record has been destroyed or falsified, every book rewritten, every picture has been repainted, every statue and street building has been renamed, every date has been altered. And the process is continuing day by day and minute by minute. History has stopped. Nothing exists except an endless present in which the Party is always right."

—George Orwell, 1984

At the Victorious Fatherland Liberation War Museum in Pyongyang, history finds a new narrative. Within the walls of this sacred space, military personnel recount tales of North Korea's struggles against its imperialist enemies—the Japanese and the Americans. Here, the Korean War is believed to have been initiated by the United States, who allegedly crossed the 38th parallel (the border between North and South Korea), on June 25, 1950. Outside of North Korea, it's a different story. Records show that seventy-five thousand soldiers from the North Korean People's Army poured across the 38th parallel and into South Korea, resulting in the start of the war.

The memorial is packed with historic weapons, "captured" American tanks, heavy machinery, and wax scenes recounting the atrocities inflicted on the North Koreans by the American troops supporting the South. Within the building there is even a 360-degree diorama of the Battle of Daejon; brave stories are told about how the North Korean and Chinese troops drove out large numbers of American and South Korean troops. The day is celebrated in the country as Victory Day, even though there was never an official winner declared, after an armistice was signed in 1953.

While Ted was restricted from making photographs within the museum, he was encouraged to show-case the exteriors in his frames. Pictured here are students of soldiers who lost their lives in battle. Soon after the making of this photograph, the photographer was taken to see one of the country's most prized possessions, the USS Pueblo. The American Navy spy vessel was seized and captured in North Korean waters in 1968. The symbol of Korean pride is on display, complete with shattered glass and large bullet holes, used as a backdrop for dramatic accounts of how it was taken, while omitting stories about the inhumane torture inflicted by the Koreans on the eighty-three crew members for eleven months.

Propaganda and the idea of war are woven into the very fabric of upbringing, and in schools teachers can be heard advising, "We must learn from Generalissimo Kim about how to hate our enemies."

80
"So, what do you do in your free time? Do you have any boyfriends or girlfriends?" asks a high-pitched voice in the background of a video Ted recorded of the Juche Tower. As he and Cheng hold back their laughter and coy smiles, their guide at the Grand People's Study House in Pyongyang is openly flirting with a tourist accompanying them in the elevator. "You're single? How? You're handsome," continues the woman, as she giggles shyly. This fairly normal encounter has stayed with Ted. North Koreans tend to marry North Koreans, so openly flirting with an international visitor seems like an anomaly.

After exiting the library elevator, Cheng asks Ri if it's usual for North Koreans to marry foreigners, to which he responds, "We can, but we don't want to." This is quite commonly heard whenever North Koreans are confronted with controversial queries. The questions you aren't allowed to ask are reveal-ing in and of themselves. Ri continues about how his Chinese tour groups frequently inquire about single women from North Korea, since they are exceptionally attractive and kind. "We have all kinds of medicine here, but no plastic surgery. Here, we are all beautiful," boasts Ri. Curiously, this is a fact contested by a North Korean defector, who reveals that she herself underwent plastic surgery before defecting from the country.

Moving away from conversations about vanity, the librarian ushers Ted into one of the six hundred rooms of the study house that is the center of Juche studies. It is said that the national library can hold up to thirty million books, and sees ten thousand students and adults per day. Apart from an array of free classes in science, technology, and the arts, students also learn English, Russian, German, and Chinese.

Ted spots multiple books by the leaders, and even stacks of Harry Potter books lying untouched in the library trolley. It's one of the few places in the country where pop culture exists so openly and can be seen in form of the voices of the Beatles emanating from the music room, or foreign fashion magazines lining the shelves. Interestingly, no religious books can be found amongst the millions available.

82-83
The basement of the International Friendship Exhibition. The photographer was asked to delete this image by an officer, and his minder.

85
Daily patrol, and casual reinforcements inscribed upon an arc that read: "I come to Mansudae Art Studio, and every time I come, I get more attached, and become more friendly."

86

Pyongyang, the land of the privileged, saw its first ever beer festival in 2016. The so-called Oktober-fest of the North was launched in hopes of promoting the government's Taedonggang Beer Factory, founded by fond drinker and former leader Kim Jong Il. It was mysteriously cancelled after the first and last event, with no explanation given. But the lack of beer festivals doesn't deter the North Koreans from gathering at the rising number of beer gardens across the country. Their specialty alcohol is a point of curiosity for many connoisseurs the world over, since the country proudly announced that their scientists have conjured up recipes for "hangover-free booze."

Every man in Pyongyang receives weekly beer coupons from the state, with which they can buy five liters of the rice beer per month. Ted visits one such garden in Pyongyang, and notices that ninety percent of the customers are men. As they sip their refreshing pints, his minders, Ri and Park, excitedly point at an allegedly famous North Korean actor and ask the photographer if he'd like to be introduced. Of course he is most intrigued, and the actor, who has apparently played a Japanese villain in many films about battling imperialist forces, is more than willing. He goes so far as to fix his hair and ensure they find the best light to work in. Funnily, when Ted later shows the photograph to a local A/V store owner, and asks about the films the actor might have made, the owner doesn't seem to recognize him.

89

The Mansudae Art Studio is a center for the study of the mediums of ink, oil, acrylic, woodcut, embroi-dery, drawing, tempera, calligraphy, watercolor, and jewel painting. Though styles may vary from artist to artist, the form is usually socialist-realist. The studio is also known to be the chief manufacturer of traditionally ink-washed Korean propaganda posters, colloquially known as *Chosonhwa*.

Fascinated by this colorful and uplifting style of artistry, Ted bought and asked Ri to mail a propagan-da-infused postcard to his friend in Hong Kong. It's been over a year, but the postcard still hasn't arrived.

90-92

> *Our father is Marshall Kim Il Sung,*
> *Our abode is the bosom of the party,*
> *We are brothers and sisters,*
> *We have nothing to envy in the world.*

> —Excerpt from a poem titled "We Are the Happiest Children
> in the World," recited at the Mangyongdae Children's Palace, Pyongyang

The first leader of North Korea, Kim Il Sung, continues to be the gentle father of the nation, twenty-six years after his demise. He once remarked, "Children are the kings of the country." In celebration of this idea, most North Korean cities have a local "children's palace" that handpicks the most gifted children in their community, and nurtures their extracurricular talents.

In Pyongyang, the Mangyongdae Children's Palace is one such institution, established on May 2, 1989, in the lead-up to the 13th World Festival of Youth and Students. Considered a testament to care and devotion by the leaders, the capital's most gifted children between eleven and sixteen years old mold themselves at this shrine to youth. Befittingly, the two wings of the facade are believed to resemble the "loving embrace of a mother." The Palace is a mandatory pit stop on North Korea's carefully crafted tours, which presumably reflect the highest aspirations of this last bastion of Stalinism.

Amidst glossy high ceilings, colorful floors, and whimsical walls plastered with flowers, planets, and stars, children learn special techniques in painting, embroidery, ballet, calligraphy, computers, and traditional and modern instruments such as the *kayagum* and accordion. There's also a pool building with a multi-tiered diving platform, and indoor basketball and volleyball courts.

While some children practice songs about how they wish every day was New Year's Day, since that's when Kim Il Sung would visit the Palace at midnight, other youngsters practice their needlepoint techniques by writing "2.16" and "10.10'"—representing February 16, the birthday of Kim Jong Il, and October 10, the day the Workers' Party was founded. On Tuesdays and Thursdays, the children showcase their talents in a forty-five-minute variety show, mostly customized for tourists and foreigners. Ted is particularly hypnotized by a little girl spinning around at incredible speed. The dance is steeped in traditional North Korean technique and extremely difficult to pull off.

Even though the photographer presumes that he might be desensitized to these sights by now, he is surprised by the armed soldiers strolling across the floor. It is a "children's" palace, after all. Here, too, the nuclear agenda is used as casual decor, and like everywhere in the country, gigantic maps portray both North and South Korea as one large nation. A distant dream, but one that's continuously enforced.

95

As the sun sets in Pyongyang, darkness descends upon the fairly deserted streets of the city. Fragmented bursts of electricity illuminate the city's monuments, stadiums, and statues of the seraphic leaders. But apart from these pillars of nationalism, a place tinted with unabashed revelry glints in shades of neon and flashing lights. It's the Kaeson Youth Park, one of two amusements parks that dot the capital of North Korea.

Every night from 7 p.m. to 11 p.m., locals, usually in their thirties, unwind at this fun fair, which is one of the few places in North Korea where foreigners can mingle with the resident comrades. The atmosphere reminds Ted of a popular computer game from the '90s named RollerCoaster Tycoon, mostly because of how far removed the environment is from the rest of the city.

Here you'll see an uninhibited version of the citizens, who let go of their disciplined body language and fairly rigid expressions to squeal, shriek, laugh, and rejoice. Since a great deal of the visitors swarm in after work, they're mostly dressed in uniform. It is apparent here that there is the person in uniform, and a different version of the person underneath it.

Apart from Italian-built rides in the form of roller coasters, carousels, drop towers, and elevated chair-swings, there is also a hamburger joint where visitors can binge on fast food. It hints at Kim Jong Un's strategy to simulate Western consumerist ideas for Pyongyang's elite, who are essential for him to stay in power.

Since a North Korean's world usually ends at the border of the nation, these islands of enjoyment are essential to elevate the citizen's morale. "We've never been abroad, but we don't think we're missing out because we have so many parks here," expresses a local, further propagating this thought. On national holidays, North Koreans can visit the parks free of charge, and they're popular spots for dates and brewing romances. Park, too, often visits with her boyfriend.

While Ted is not a big fan of rides at amusement parks, he decides to partake in the bumper cars. Unsurprisingly, riding bumper cars in North Korea comes with a twist: the aim of the game is to avoid getting bumped, instead of doing the bumping.

114

The country of North Korea legitimizes the idea that borders exist as much in our minds as they do on geographical maps. This is not to claim that demarcations might stifle the ones who believe in them, but to acknowledge how ideology permeates every aspect of a North Korean's life. As their ancestry drips with carefully crafted formulae, you realize that there might exist a fine line between genuine belief and genuine fear. These are the thoughts of an outsider living in a "normal" vastly different from theirs.

The comrades remain oblivious to Kim Jong Un's Swiss education, or the historic handshake between their beloved general and their nemesis, Donald Trump, which took place in Singapore in 2018. They are blissfully unaware of how Kim Jong Il's hair was cut in a certain way so that he would appear taller, or that the Korean War was, indeed, initiated by them. The belief that their leaders are infallible governs their every move. Lovingly, they are their leaders, and their leaders are them.

Every single day, North Korean citizens dutifully strive toward economic, cultural, and individual growth within an authoritarian system that controls their growing. But as Ted says, we may come in with our own biases, and leave realizing that this is their world.

It's curious though, that at Moranbong, people are encouraged to pay any amount they'd like to release a cage of pigeons, coincidentally giving physical form to the thought that, in North Korea, freedom exists, but not without a price.

– Zahra Amiruddin

ACKNOWLEDGMENTS

From Ted:
For their hospitality and for showing me their country, thank you to Ri, Park, and Kim. Thank you to Michael Itkoff for giving me this opportunity; to Chris Lee and Tim Lee for their encouragement and support; and to Yu-Ting Cheng, Daniel Huete, and Zahra Amiruddin for their invaluable input and collaboration.

From Zahra:
For helping me understand the mysteries of North Korea with unbiased eyes, thank you to Daniel Jasper, Janice Yeonjin Kim, and Sung Hyung Cho, exceptional documentary filmmaker of *My Brothers and Sisters in the North*.

A heartfelt shoutout to Daniel Huete for his belief, and of course, Ted Lau, for his faith, trust, and endless conversations.

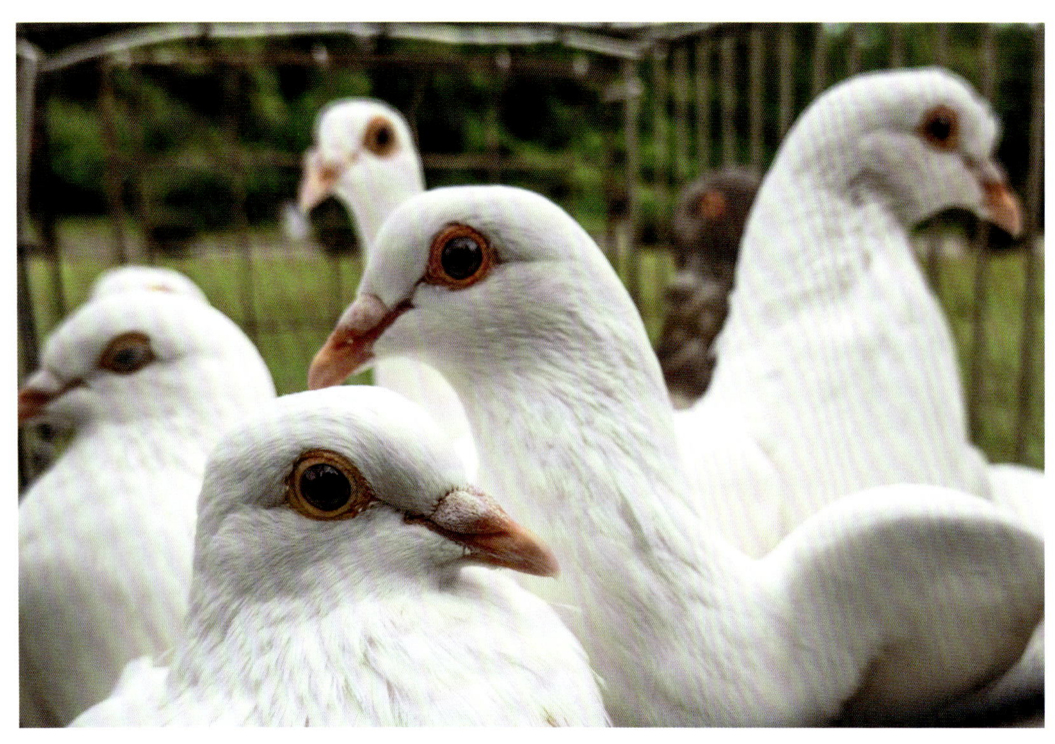